ANCESTOR
NETWORKING

CHARLES SPENCER KING

DEDICATION

My father is with the ancestors and before he departed he shared with me the story of my grandfather, Charles George King who was born in Wales and whose mother was widowed. She remarried a man named Henry King from Cornwall, England. Therefore my name really is not King at all, and this is particularly important with our ancestors. For example many African Americans adopted the name of the plantation owner and while that may be the name of some recent ancestors; it is not the name of their African ancestors. It is important to know the names of our ancestors as far back as possible so we can honor them and connect with them. Therefore, I dedicate this book to my ancestors on my paternal grandfather's side, by the name of Cottle.

CONTENTS

Who am I?

I'm a senior Baba Awo in the Cuban Lucumi culture who is an author and specializes in education and exposing fraud, abuses and I study dreams. We will delve deeper into what is a Babalawo and Baba Awo and what is

Cuban Lucumi as we go. Lucumi is a branch or sect of the West African and Yoruba people who are mostly in southern Nigeria, Benin and Cameroon. Latin America and The Diaspora is full of these descendants who first arrived on slave ships. Although my study is primarily Lucumi, I also study many Latin American cultures and beliefs, many from India, China, Japan, Native American and other indigenous peoples throughout the world.

My destiny in Lucumi is for global education as opposed to most Babalawo who educate and serve clients one at a time. I have no godchildren, students or clients in Lucumi. I mostly lecture and write. Recently I have begun to help a very select and few individuals to begin their journey to connect with their ancestors and The Dead. Unfortunately, there is but one of me and many find my session rate to be excessive, but the demand is high and value justifies the price. Others find it a bargain. You can find my session rates at the end of the book. Why am I sharing this in a book? The book provides a foundation, logic and knowledge to share the keys for you to understand, it is a first step in a process. Sorry, I wish I could snap my fingers and impart all your connections onto you, but it does not work that way.

Make no mistake; there are benefits as you go forward in the process. Think of the process like a battery that needs to be charged. Perhaps you understand the basics of ancestor veneration or based forms of Yoruba. Maybe you are Hindu, Shinto, Buddhist, or gifted in meditation, yoga or chakra. Possibly you are knowledgeable of Nature based beliefs, indigenous, pagan or a spiritualist. These all can help greatly to build your foundation. Within both the ancestor and The Dead components of spirituality there is unlimited protection, knowledge and power to be accessed and this book will help get you started with your foundation. You'll see I do not need to hover over you to help you; it is a little like management by objectives, but without a time limit. Some are quicker than others in getting their foundation built. I do not coddle you or punish you if you do not get the homework done or if it takes you years rather than months, this is all up to you. I will lead you to the water; but whether or not you drink is up to you.

Some are scared of The Dead and some should be scared of The Dead, but understanding them should make you less scared. Same with our ancestors and sure I can teach you to repair a negative relationship with either, but again you have to do the work, I won't push you. What I can assure you of is that learning about these spirits will not endanger you anymore than you already are; thus it is a win – win situation for you.

Finally, indeed there are many, many hoaxes, cons, frauds and that ilk. However there are some who have the gift in all different disciplines. Maybe they can do an accurate chart for you, channeling or any other forms of divination or spiritual guidance. I am not an expert of all, I am a student of many, and most underwhelm me. I am going to help you build with this book what works over time when and IF you follow the steps. I would say based on my experience with others it works completely with about 30% of open minded people (after the foundation is built) and another 50% get significant improvement and value from the process (after the foundation is built). About 20% are in denial and get little benefit (of those who commit themselves) to the process.

This book is not an opus, it is a primer. Nor is it the biggest or longest book I have authored; but good things can come in small packages. These pages could change your life or it could open a door that overwhelms you. One thing it won't be is a regurgitated hodgepodge of other books on the subject. I like interacting with my readers on Facebook or on the site where I have many free articles Academia.com, so do stop by and say hello!

ANCESTOR NETWORKING

Forward:

It is not a secret how to venerate and pray to our ancestors, Ancestor Worship is the largest belief in world culture, spirituality and religion and always has been. Many teach this in many different forms. The challenge is the conversation is a one way street; you're talking, praying, asking and you get no answer! This book (believe it or not) will actually share how to get real answers, how to hear their voices and how to improve your spirituality and life by incorporating your ancestor's advice into your life. Tall order? Come on inside, let me show you how to begin!

CHARLES SPENCER KING

Chapter One:

The first item I want to make very clear is whatever religion or spirituality you are, this book can help you. If you are agnostic or even atheist, this book can help you connect with departed spirits via Nature. The book is more than simple ancestor veneration and communication, and if you care to you can throw everything else we discuss out the window (or not pursue it) and still develop a significant connection with your ancestors by practicing the methods outlined here. Almost everyone can improve their communicating to our ancestors and improve or recognize how our ancestors communicate with us. Learning how to send and receive communications will significantly improve your relationship with your ancestors.

Unlike most religions, cultures and spirtualties that are faith based, this book is not. Therefore you have the option to disconnect the teachings from religion if you choose to. You can be Hindu, Christian, Muslim, Buddhist, Yoruba, Pagan, Shinto, Native or a non-believer and I will teach you how to understand the basics of developing a relationship and two way street with your ancestors. You might wonder why if this is true, how you have not heard of it before. I don't really have an answer for that, maybe I stumbled across it or it fell into my lap, perhaps it is some ancient wisdom that I pieced together. I've remembered my dreams from about age four; but I don't view it as a unique gift. Many will scream "bullshit" even before they read the book, and yeah I might too, if I suddenly read I could send and receive messages from the dead. I am not writing this to sell you on what I have learned; knowledge is something that we either pursue or we ignore; the choice is yours. One thing is that it is a process that was not learned overnight for me, it took years to develop it and I am far from having all the answers. However I can and will get you started.

I'll lay this out for you from the Cuban Lucumi based knowledge that I specialize in, but you can apply it to any form of religion, culture or spirituality. The book is more than just ancestor veneration as I said, but please bear with me as I explain it in my own imperfect way. Please understand that I am not an expert in all forms of religion and when I use examples (other than Lucumi) they may not be perfect. I use them to help everyone identify with whatever their individual religion, culture or spirituality is and sometimes I may do so poorly; for this I apologize in advance. My intention is not to disrespect anyone's belief system. Finally in my opinion (particularly with ancestor veneration and communication) this methodology is a compliment not a substitute for your system.

Rather than start with the ancestors we want to provide you with some tools or you might say frame the discussion. When we pray, venerate or proportion a deity or a spirit (any spirit) it is a one way street, we plead; and they listen (hopefully). It can be Lord Vishnu, Jesus, Olodumare, Al- Rhaman, Wheguru, The Creator or many more. We also pray to sub deities like Orishas, an avatar of a

God, los muertos or The Dead, a saint, angel, ancestors, a force or element of Nature; really the list is long. We assume they are listening and hopefully grant our wishes or pleas. Some cultures feed them food, give them gifts, honor them with gifts in their name; others seek to make a deal, such as "If you do this for me, I promise I will do this for you". All of these methods may or may not work, for example maybe God already knows what we need or want.

I don't hear many credible people claiming to have conversations with any spirits of deities and this is why I call it a one way street. When we do hear someone claim that God, a deity or a spirit spoke to them we tend to raise an eyebrow. Usually we hear of people receiving a sign like the virgin weeping or Lord Shiva making Mount Kailash change colors or Mount Yoshino for the Shinto or something of that nature. In many cases we find shrines or holy places in Nature, the river Ganges, a totem pole in a forest, a mountain temple, or the sacred shells of the Yoruba.

Nature and our relationship with it is a key that some cultures embrace while others largely ignore or take for granted. Pope Francis to his credit seems to be more active in reestablishing this important link with Nature. Many Latinos understand the importance of Nature and often address it with supplementing their Catholicism with either a mezzo American set of beliefs, African or one from an India based religion. Not to pick on my Catholic pals, but it has long puzzled me and others why not one of The Ten Commandments address Nature. The fact that there are no sins or transgressions against Nature to atone for in the confessional is puzzling. Certainly God did not forget Nature and most find it hard to believe that it would be more important to not covet in three commandments than respecting Nature. We will discuss Nature in depth later. But let me

add that there are many good things about
Judaism, Christianity and Islam, but reverence
for Nature is not an apparent one.

Let's start with a few concepts that will
frame the big picture for you. The first is the
soul, atman, ori Ruh, nephesh, hun and po,
divine spirit etc. Basically this is something
that our human bodies host and it goes on
after the body has expired. The human body
we all have a pretty good knowledge of so we
do not need to explain that. Many cultures
believe in a Natural energy that has a
connection or flows from Nature. The Yoruba
for instance call this ase or in The Diaspora
(such as Cuba) ashe. Ashe is a positive energy
that with knowledge we can acquire through
things like love, family, gifts to Nature, noble
deeds etc. All Natural things including Man
have ashe, a rock, tree, water, shells etc.
Furthermore there are two types of ashe, one
is temporal for the life of the human body and
the other is more permanent for the soul.

Obviously the permanent one is more difficult to earn. The concept is the more ashe we acquire, the better life is.

The last component is balance; we see almost every culture value balance highly. For example ashe is positive and on the other side of the scale is juju that is negative. Or it could be Yin and Yang, many cultures embrace this concept. There are several other concepts such as Heaven and Hell or Purgatory but we are getting off on a tangent and my goal is to lightly discuss these major concepts in the first chapter.

Now let's continue with the deities. When I speak of a deity my focus is very narrow, it means God. In many cultures there are many Gods, some are avatars, others are for and do specific tasks, most are either connected, represent or can manipulate forces or elements of Nature. All God's are immortal from my studies; even though they may have died, been reborn and died again, like Jesus, so let's just say that their soul is immortal to be more accurate. God or Gods are certainly more powerful than humans, so we will put them all on the top rung or at the apex of whatever spirituality you practice.

In many cultures there are subservient Gods, I don't like to use "lesser" as I would not want to insult any. Some of these are sons, daughters, demi gods, avatars. In the Yoruba for instance Olodumare is the creator and he is largely unavailable as he is off creating other dimensions, time lines, universes etc. He left two avatars of himself to rule our universe before he took off. These are Olorun: who lives in the sky and like the rainbow never touches earth; and Olofin who is of both sky and Earth who does visit regularly. Both Olorun and Olofin are God and Olofin for example shared his ashe and this made the Earth's oceans, rivers, plants, animals etc.

Below these Gods are the immortal Orishas in Lucumi, most of the 201 Orishas have an element of Nature they can manipulate. The Orisha is not the natural element or force but more like a guardian. Interestingly like the Christians or Muslims most praying to God is through the Orishas just like Muslims often use Mohammed or Christians pray to Jesus or through the Holy Ghost to get to God. Many cultures have a buffer like this as opposed to proportioning God(s) direct. Native Americans might pray through a natural element or a sacred animal or bird to The Creator. In Hinduism one popular belief is that there are 33 million deities (33 crore)!

The Yoruba have four columns or conduits to God they are A) The Dead, B) The Ancestors C) The Orishas and D) IFA divination. Followers can get to God through any of the four columns and theoretically each of the four has equal power. Again, I use the philosophy that none is "lesser". We still have not heard from

God or his servants yet have we? But we have filled our one way street with quite a few different vehicles. The reason I keep coming back to the Yoruba or Lucumi hierarchy is because I want to teach you using this. It is quite simple, ancient and has the important connection with Nature. It is also fairly easy to envision whatever your belief system is into it.

I think we are ready to show you that there are vehicles moving on the same street in the other direction. Permit me to over simplify in saying when we are awake and alive we have a consciousness. We also have a subconscious that most often is associated with altered states such as dreaming, or deep meditation. There are such things as waking dreams, daydreams or trance but these we'll discuss later as the lion's share of subconscious is while we are asleep. In fact about one third of our life is spent sleeping. Science also informs us that everyone dreams; whether they remember or not when they wake up. Rather than put the book down if you are one of those who can't remember your dreams; let me assure you that anyone can be trained to remember their dreams and improve on the memory if you don't remember well. I'll give you the keys to improve what you remember.

The first step is to understand and categorize just who can enter your dreams. Certainly the omniscient God or Gods can enter your dreams at will; but I've not heard of God or Gods entering our dreams too often. Should God enter your dream he (or she) has the power to make you remember the dream. It is more common (though still rare) for say The Buddha, Mohammad, Krishna, Jesus, Matsu, Orishas or other immortals to enter your dreams. More common still it is one of our ancestors or a member of The Dead who visit.

We are still qualifying and categorizing for clarities sake. Perhaps your question is what is the difference between The Dead and your ancestors? That is a good question with not so easy of answer, so let's attack it before moving on. Yes, our ancestors are dead and technically the ancestors are part of The Dead, but the two have very different functions we should discuss. First and foremost both are or were humans and because they were each has limitations that immortals or deities do not have. The most important of these is that a dead spirit (or an ancestor) cannot be in multiple locations at the same time like an immortal or deity.

This is quite important to digest and understand because suppose you are praying to one and they are with another of your relatives, your message might not get through, unlike with an immortal or deity. They can also be called away, remember they do not have special powers like an immortal or deity. They are also on the bottom of the totem pole in rank, they serve deities and immortals, and thus they can be called away. Understanding any dead spirit's limitations is important and we'll discuss these in depth later. Absolutely they have knowledge and advice to share (if and when they are willing though).

What's the difference between a member of The Dead and our ancestors? Think of The Dead as any spirit that is not an ancestor. OK, what defines an ancestor? There are three types of ancestors, the first we all know and call our blood ancestors. The second type of ancestor is one who we share DNA and MT haplogroup mapping with and the third is what we call an ashe or lineage ancestor. The first two are fairly self-explanatory while lineage ancestors are more complex. In the many African cultures including Yoruba and in some other cultures ashe is shared through various ceremonies. Other cultures might not call it ashe, many use Nature's energy for example; but it is either very similar or it is the same.

The first step is recognizing its existence,

However even if we do not, we still are able to acquire ashe as I pointed out earlier. Therefore one is not required to change their faith just to acquire ashe, anyone can. Surely, once we recognize its existence it is easier to acquire. Have you ever felt drawn to a stick in a forest, a rock on a plateau, a shell on the beach or a tree on a river's bank or a stone in a brook? When we are drawn to these Natural things it is usually their ashe luring us to make contact so the transfer can be made. Acquiring ashe is an ability we all have whether it is conscious or subconscious. Passing on ashe to others is much more difficult and usually requires training.

Yet not always, for example a healer can and does share their ashe with you even if they are not aware of it. Lovers or children can and do share their ashe without recognizing it. Nature does the same thing for us. Even science admits there is a form of energy throughout Nature. How lineage ashe works is it is given by the leader of various ceremonies as I mentioned. In the Yoruba culture there are two sides (again balance) of their culture, one is through divination and the Orisha of divination is named Orunmila or Orula. The flip side is called ocha or Orisha worship and both have lineage ashe we can acquire. On both sides this connects us to lineage ancestors.

Even though these leaders were mortal, they all have abundant knowledge and power because they were leaders when alive. The ashe comes from the first ancestors generationally to the one receiving it through ceremony. Outsiders don't require lineage ashe; but it is very useful. Why is it useful? Because this long line of ancestors are all powerful practitioners, so compared to a blood or DNA ancestor they have much more knowledge to share with us in the dream world or astral planes. We'll discuss these more later on!

Our categories then are A) God or the principal deities B) the sub deities or immortals C) The Dead (los muertos) and D) Our Ancestors. Not too complex is it? All of these can speak to you in your dreams, but it is mostly our ancestors and The Dead who do. The next assumption we can make is that our ancestors usually are our biggest advocates. Your ancestors want to help you (assuming you are good). There are occasionally negative ancestors and having one is a relationship that needs to be repaired (and it can be). For the most part we can look at our ancestors as being our biggest fans or allies in the dream world. Because The Dead is such a large group and because of balance there are many more negative spirits in the dream world we must consider and protect ourselves from.

Chapter Two:

The previous chapter we introduced several topics, now let's see if we can make some sense of them by providing you with some visuals. We discussed the one way street and how we ask for things when we are awake or conscious and we explained some of the limitations such as a spirit (ancestor or one of The Dead). What I'd like to introduce next is another visual that may be useful. Hopefully this can advance your understanding significantly. You've finally fallen asleep where are you? We always start in the same place I like to call our castle. The castle is your stronghold, base, safe place; think of it just like a castle. It has substantial defenses, a moat, think high walls, ramparts and it is manned with your army. Your army is your ancestors be they blood, DNA or lineage. Your ancestors do not leave the castle, even if you do, they stay and they keep your castle safe awaiting your return.

The only other inhabitants are your spiritual guides, think of these as your away party or the battle hardened warriors that accompany you when you leave the security of your castle.

Most people have between three and seven spiritual guides and one of these is at your side 24 hours a day, seven days a week and certainly anytime you are asleep. The others may spend time with you in your castle but are mainly used when we mount our steed and gallop out of the castle or take a walk outside the castle walls. What or who exactly is a spiritual guide?

Many cultures recognize these protective spirits, the key is how to identify them and build a relationship with them. The Yoruba in Nigeria call these spirits egbe and they are learned and received through ceremony and anytime we mention ceremony there is a cost. One of the great things about Cuban Lucumi is learning who our spiritual guides are if free of charge in Lucumi, however not in Nigeria. Other cultures can also find out who at least some of these are for free and once you have identified a guide, then you can build a relationship with them. The guides however are not part of our ancestors; they are part of The Dead.

In Cuban Lucumi and other cultures they are identified in several ways and confirmed. The most common way is through a spiritual misa. This is a bit like a séance except there is no crystal ball. During a misa a spirit takes possession of a person or persons at the misa and they give advice and act as a link between the conscious and unconscious or spirt world. The main problem with a misa is there are many fake ones and we will come back to that revelation pronto. Not only could a member of The Dead or ancestors take possession but also it could be an immortal Orisha. The Lucumi community is very open to allowing anyone to attend a misa. In Cuba or other parts of Latin America such as Brazil or Venezuela where the culture is strong it is easy to find a misa. Some do charge a nominal fee though and what I mean by nominal is less than 100.00 USD. Normally they are free of charge though and I (personally) would not trust one that charged more than $100. Of course we can also throw our own misa but even this can be done for normally less than $100 – 300USD. The advantage of throwing our own is the spirit or Orisha that is possessing spends more time with us than the other guests. The spirit tends to talk with everyone, but not always; therefore it might take several misas to discover your guides.

The second way to find a spiritual guide is to attend a tambor. A tambor is is a festive occasion honoring a Orisha replete with music (usually drumming), dancing and general revelry. The tambor is usually given by one or several practitioners, who either wish to ask the Orisha for something, thank them for something or simply honor them. Most Orisha as we mentioned have a Natural element or force they are associated with, interestingly they also have unique colors, numbers and a drum rhythm or beat that is unique to them.

Depending on the tradition, for example in Cuban Lucumi the Orisha Eleggua's colors are red and black, his number is three and any multiple of three (particularly 21).His beat (or any other Orisha) you can find on You Tube.

Possession (or mounting as the Cubans call it) is controversial largely because there are fakes. But I can assure you it can be very real and when it is real we can learn a bunch of useful information and most importantly who our guides are. I have never been mounted mostly because of how I grew in this culture. I will share some of this in the next chapters when I take excerpts from my book *Nature's Ancient Religion: Orisha Worship and IFA* to illustrate my personal relationship in the culture. My rank of Babalawo or any priest of IFA cannot be mounted, thus the window of opportunity closed quickly; in my case when I went from being a cynic to thinking there might just be something in all this hocus pocus. My book, NAR is about 40%

autobiography and that 40% outlines my early journey from non-believer and cynic to Babalawo or father of secrets as the word translates to.

Because I was such an analytical cynic for so long (and still am) I understand it is not easy for most readers to buy in to the concept of possession or mounting. I was more than skeptical too and in fact in my role as exposing fraud and abuse I still encounter many fakes. But for now you'll just have to trust me that some possession is very real. We can also open this up a bit by reminding you in other cultures that possession is real, if we look at the negative side of it in Christianity for example that requires exorcism. Most cultures including Christianity believe in possession. Let's also use balance again as not all possession is negative or harmful angels in Christianity also can possess or mount a subject. All African traditions and indigenous religions believe in possession; Islam, Hinduism, Sikhism,

Buddhism, Chinese folk, Shinto, Wicca include possession.

The third method for determining our spiritual guides is less hocus pocus and more logic. Cultures like my White American pals or those who wish to segregate this outside of religion can utilize this method rather than the first two. The reality is most well-adjusted whites run from anything that resembles witchcraft or what Latinos call brujeria or in India is known as shamanism. The challenge with this method is you'll need to be able to remember large swaths of your dreams before you can employ it. For most, this takes a bit of training or knowledge, but not to worry we will cover how to improve your memory later.

The third method is recognizing habitual presences in your dreams. If a person (who is dead) frequents your dreams, chances are excellent they are a guide. Logical isn't it? To a lesser extent this can also be an indication when someone pops into our head while we are awake as in day dreaming, but this is trickier to ascertain. Still it is an indication and when combined with the information in the dream can be a reasonable indication. The other thing to remember is ancestors are never guides. In fact it is very rare for any of your guides to be people you encountered in your life who died; most guides are several to many generations apart from us.

In Cuban Lucumi and other cultures we always confirm the guide. This is done through various forms of divination and again there are frauds who claim to be gifted diviners who are not, so having knowledge is essential. The Lucumi have several methods of divination, a few are relatively simple and others are more complex. Shaman, guru or qualified medicine men (and women) can also confirm through various forms of divination. Meditation and yoga can help. In the end it is no disaster if you can't confirm or even if a fraud confirms something not real. This is just is a waste of your time and energies, but it does not really hurt you, and yeah it sure does not help you either.

Why are the guides so important? We can live in our castle and never leave, but the inquisitive nature of Man is not big on resting on our laurels in stagnation. We like to get out, live, love, learn. Suppose you live in a high rise in the center of a city, like Chicago. Sure you can stay inside and order in anything you need, but most of us go out while we are active. The fact is though that whenever you leave your building for the street, danger is lurking. Indeed there are great rewards to be found outside your building but there is also danger. The simple fact is there is safety in numbers. Perhaps the bigger and more important fact is in the dream or spirit world we are more vulnerable to attack.

Think of it like this: you are in a coma in

your house or a hospital or you are in a coma on the street. Because when we are asleep we have little control as opposed to when we are awake. You may now wonder if we can learn to be in control when we are asleep; the answer is yes, definitely yes. However this is more advanced and requires either a rare gift or a whole lot of training and knowledge. Let me share an experience from my childhood. When I was four I began remembering my dreams; my sister and friends could not with the same clarity, my brother thoug had a talent for dreaming. I dream normally in grayscale, but occasionally in color and at four years old this was before color television was introduced. Remembering our dreams well is an advantage, but like I explained earlier this can be taught also. What the real gift for me was, having a running serial in my dreams. In fact it was not one serial, it was four. I would wake up every morning with Quick Draw McGraw, Diver Dan, Speedy Gonzales or Buggs Bunny cartoons fresh in my head. I had no control of which it would be, but always one, every night and I was in kindergarten. Maybe even more interesting was the fact that my dream started at the last scene of the previous episode. Oddly it was never scenes from the actual shows on television, but new and fresh ones. After about a year and a half I still dreamed of the four but not every night. Over the next year I stopped dreaming these.

Now I have never had anything like this occur since, otherwise I would be packaging it to sell! Yet it is odd and it forced me to consider much later in life when I had earned the opportunity to choose a specialty of Lucumi for my studies. Dreams became my specialty in Lucumi. It is not a mainstream specialty though and finding mentors and knowledge was not easy, yet eight years later I am glad I choose it (or it chose me).

Sorry about the tangent, but we need to get back to the question of why the spiritual

guides are important. Few people have any
control over their dreams and when we are
asleep either we are dreaming or we are
resting without dreams. We rarely need
protection in our castle; but when we leave the
castle to explore we do need it. The Dead are
good and bad, evil and righteous; some have
agendas, others would not lift a finger to help
you; some do not like your looks or how you
speak or walk, just like the real world when we
are awake. We are more vulnerable in the
dream world because we are not awake with
all of our talents and faculties, we are asleep.

Our guides are our entourage, our team
who protects and advises us. Going out alone
or without the ability to communicate on the
journey with our team is a risk. All humans
including the non-religious have guides
assigned to us, and yep they will protect us
when we leave the castle. Having a clear
objective and strategy and being able to
communicate with our guides is desirable and

a tremendous advantage over those who do not. When we recognize the existence of the dream world and its opportunities we grow spiritually. Science tells us we only use around ten percent of the brain when we are conscious. Science also tells us when we are asleep and dreaming we use more than ten percent. Should logic not tell us that the unconscious state is at least as important as the conscious state? We spend billions of dollars traveling for a few steps on the moon; but we give up on exploring the unconscious state. Part of the problem is organized religion and science seems to be competitors when they should be colleagues. Through the ages religion has sought to explain what science could not and when a discovery is made in science, organized religion often has the book already printed and it is incorrect. In fact it is a bit like anthropology or archeology in this way; a discovery is made, the book or finding is written and something later comes along that supplants it. The problem is the dated material that is proved false is still out there being read. Religious texts often face this challenge.

This resistance to education and discovery is a great weakness of organized religion. Organized religion has many strengths and positives but being progressive is not one of these. The other fact is that it is not just science that organized religions compete with; they compete with other organized religions. For example each religion has a creation story; not all of them can be correct! My objective is not to force you to accept my religion or criticize yours, like I said the knowledge in this book is primarily West African based in Cuba, however it drinks liberally from many glasses such as Hinduism and its children Buddhism, Sikhism, Jainism and indigenous cultures such as Native American. The book embraces Nature and science as well.

Personally, I do not like to think of the

information and knowledge I am sharing is
religion or science, it is somewhere in between.
I am trying to present it in a way that
compliments any and all religions and cultures
but does not try to supplant them. I am not
suggesting your relationship with your
ancestors and The Dead should or will replace
your religion or philosophy; but it certainly can
at least augment it. The fact is, I prefer to
keep this knowledge separate from the many
branches of religion. Did you know that
ancestor veneration or worship is by far the
largest theological belief in the world and
always has been? However it is not considered
a standalone religion, way of life or philosophy.
One reason why in my opinion is because
hooking up with our blood ancestors is free!
There is no monetary incentive for an
organized religion to incorporate ancestor
veneration, is there? I do not seek to change
this, I do not want to be the founder of a new
religion; in truth I am not the original author of
many of the methods and beliefs I share; in

truth I have complied them from science, philosophy and religion. It would be unfair and incorrect to credit me for this ancient knowledge.

What this knowledge can do is empower you. You do not need a church, temple or holy man or woman to guide you. Try to think of it as a beginning not an end.

CHARLES SPENCER KING

Chapter Three:

We touched upon the hocus pocus a bit and I
thought rather than to tell my story again off

the cuff I will lead in with a full chapter of my book *Nature's Ancient Religion.* This should not only share some background information you might find useful, but also share an important ceremony from a novice gringo non believer. I'm including it for flavor and background but also for a lead in to a second chapter on dreams from my book, *NAR*. These won't really give you the nuts and bolts or what we call the mechanics, but by sharing the two chapters it will give you a bit on me and how I became hooked.

The lead in or set up is, I had been spending three to four months in Cuba for the prior thirteen years. I certainly was well aware of Lucumi and avoided it like the plague, because my American culture runs from things like witchcraft or pagan beliefs. A couple years earlier I had married a Cuban doctor and she like most Cubans was active in the culture or religion if you will. The culture was also a reason for my divorce and (as you can imagine) that did not make me anymore accepting to the culture; in fact I was bitter and blamed the culture to a large extent. Several years before I had broken my back (L4 burst) and heel in a snow skiing accident and did a very successful rehab in Cuba.

Chapter Two:

Mano de Orula

I mentioned my back was killing me, and it wasn't only regressing, it was getting progressively worse. Oddly, the closer I was getting to my trip (to Cuba), the more it hurt. This made me all the more motivated to get to Niurka (My Cuban therapist) and my therapy. When I made my reservations at my travel agency, I started getting shooting pains in my back. Sitting on the bus on my way to Hermosillo,(Mexico) from Nogales, where I live, it became worse; I was Popping Aleve and Advil like candy. I spent a restless night and made it to Mexico City for the two-hour wait, hurting. By the time I arrived in Cuba that afternoon, I was limping and feeling old. I still managed to see Amado and Yoshi, his wife, and I called Rosa and Niurka. Niurka came the next day, as did Rosa, and both were concerned at the sight of me in pain. Niurka questioned me, thinking I had joined a circus act because my back was in such awful shape. When I responded that I hadn't done anything unusual, she was puzzled.

I really wanted to visit Popi (Amado's Dad) and give him the gift of the vitamins I had brought for him. For some reason, vitamins are hard to get in Cuba, another thing we can blame the embargo on. The problem with visiting Popi was that it was on the fourth floor (third in Latin America). With my back as bad *as it was, I had little hope of making it. Popi is a second father to me, and he and my biological father had a ball when Dad was down for my wedding. These two are lady-killers, and love the chase.*

I was delighted when Rosa came back into my bedroom and told me that Popi was in the living room. He also looked concerned at the sight of my now excruciating pain. Popi speaks no English, and sometimes I don't get all that he says. He told me in very serious terms that he wanted me to see his other high priests (Babalawo) as he was sure that my back problems were witchcraft (Brujaria). Yeah right, I winced. Now remember, Santeria was something that I was now vehemently against. Here was my Cuban father telling me in no uncertain terms that it was the cause of my pain. We talked and talked, and I was almost blue in the face, but he was relentless in his appraisal.

Amado and Yoshi had joined us now, and I tried reasoning through them, but nope, Popi was still relentlessly on me. Rosa, also a believer, was nodding, while even Niurka, who wasn't a believer suggested that maybe I should go. I was outnumbered and out-reasoned. Me, the great debater, defeated. I was desperate, heck, I could barely walk! We must have talked for two hours and still I wasn't in agreement, so I used the old corporate delay strategy, and said I would sleep on it.

The next day, Niurka finished and my back was slightly better, but nowhere near what I had hoped for. Good grief, Popi was at the door again! Finally, I grudgingly agreed and asked the price of all of this. He said I was family and it wasn't a matter of price, he offered to pay it himself! Now that is really something for a Cuban to do; Cubans don't have a bunch of disposable income like you and me.

We discussed it more deeply, and he reminded me of my earlier interest to find out which Orisha was my guardian angel, in other words, who was my mother or father Orisha. He informed me that the best value was to do a ceremony known as the Mano de Orula, and that they would combine a ceremony known as the Warriors, and we would also find out if it was indeed witchcraft that was affecting my back. Furthermore, I would not only know who my father or mother Orisha was, I would also know the path or road that was to be my destiny. Now, all of this seemed completely absurd to me at the time, and I was certainly not looking for any of this. All I was doing, as I saw it, was appeasing my Cuban father. I had exactly zero faith that any of this was going to matter, or cure my aching back. He shared with me that the ceremonies were over three days, but the second day was just a day of rest and herbal baths, so actually two days. The price wasn't a price for a tourist: it was $150.00. I felt like saying when I heard this,

"Are you kidding?" Four Babalawos and Popi working for at least six hours a day, and food and beverages, it seemed like a deal.

The following day, I went to meet Popi's Godfather, who was an old Babalawo named Antonio. Antonio lived in a suburb of Havana that was about twenty-five minutes from Centro Habana where we were located. Antonio was of the Matanzas branch of Santeria. He had a very nice, well-kept, large home with a lovely garden in the back. I'm not going to give his full name because there were problems, which we will get into later. I sat down and spent about an hour with Antonio, as Popi protectively looked over my shoulder. Popi and I had discussed at length over the years the manipulation that was rapidly becoming a part of Santeria. I was naturally concerned about my ceremony turning into a smoke and mirrors act; I figured if I was going to do this, I wanted to do it right without any hocus-pocus. Having Popi next to me at least made fraud a lot more unlikely. Popi assured me that the Padrino (Godfather) had plenty of experience, and had been a Babalawo for forty years.

Antonio was very affable as he got into the reading. He was using a divination device known as the Opele. This is explained in more detail in later chapters, but it is an object developed in Africa, where Orisha worship started, and is exclusively a tool of the Babalawo. Those below the rank of Babalawo are forbidden to use this object.

Basically, the interview from my perspective was him flipping this Opele a bunch of times, and jotting down stuff in a notebook. This was a consultation, not any ceremony. My ceremony was to be in two days' time in the same location. We thanked him and paid him by putting the 150 CUC on the floor a short time into my consultation. I said thanks and goodbye, and limped out of the house with the cane I was now forced to use. Popi seemed pleased, and at least he had stopped giving me a lecture on me moving forward with this "cure". Amado met us at my house, and chatted with Popi at length, while I moaned about my back to Yoshi.

My crew was Popi, and Amado, as I arrived doubled over in pain two days later. Amado sometimes wasn't allowed in the room as certain parts of the two ceremonies were exclusively for Babalawos, and Amado wasn't of that rank. Joined by Popi and Antonio were two other Babalawos; one guy I really liked was the ever-smiling Jose. Jose seemed to perform most of the various things I did. It was mostly just me sitting in a chair with my bare feet on a mat, either answering questions or shaking two small shells or stones in my hand, and Jose grabbing a bunch of palm seeds from his hand, ending up with either one or two seeds. He would then mark either one or two marks on a wooden plate carved with odd objects. The plate had an orange looking powder on it. I did other things like name my family members a few times, and watched the

Babalawos do some chanting outside in the garden and inside as well, but really, I was lost most of the time; totally clueless with what was going on.

I eventually learned that my father was Aggayu the Orisha of the Volcano, and I chuckled at this as I do have a temper. I had been told I could either find out who my father or my mother was, but not both, and I had opted for my father. I learned a little about the strange statue of the head that was Eshu, or Eleggua, who was the messenger of the other Orishas, and keeper of the crossroads. I also received an iron pot with some metal objects and stones that represented Oggun the Orisha of Iron, and his brother Ochoshi the divine hunter. The oddest object I received was a metal rooster on what seemed to be a covered goblet. These Orishas make up the Warriors. Orula (Orunmila) is naturally received during the Mano or Cofa de Orula ceremony that we were combining. I remember it took a long time to find out that Aggayu was my father.

We took some breaks and ate well during these ceremonies, and throughout all this, my back was still hurting. I remember complaining to Popi that we had gone through the first day and my back was still hurting. He told me to be patient and the answer and solution would come the second day. Amado was explaining to me the 256 paths that each person is born with, while we went through a long process to find this out.

I watched Jose work the palm seeds, and saw the anxious faces of all that were there. These guys were literally on the edge of their seats at this point. By the time the seventh mark was made, the youngest Babalawo was really excited, and Jose and Antonio were sharing grins with Popi. Me? I was lost and had no idea what was causing them this amusement. Of course, later I learned that because there are only eight marks; after the seventh there are only two possibilities, and any seasoned Babalawo knows these two before the last mark is made. Well, I had my sign or my road or path, and all seemed pleased. It was the sign known as Irso Meji (Melli). This was all explained to me by each of the Babalawos, who took turns telling me about me.

Now, I had a girlfriend who I loved very dearly, she was a news commentator, and is still a columnist for the Chicago Sun Times. Her name is Mary. Mary was quite gaga about the spiritual side of things. In the four years we were joined at the hip, she dragged me to plenty of spiritualists. I had my horoscope done by Sidney Omar and Jean Dixon. We saw Uri Geller and Barbara Comarte. Ms. Comarte was the wildest and the most accurate, she was famous for predicting Oprah would leave Philadelphia when she still had a radio talk show there, and move to Chicago and be a huge success. Through Mary, I had my spiritual awakening, and I took these with more than a grain of salt for the most part. My friend Indu recently had the top astrologist in India do my stars, and that was also nice, but most of *these things are too general to be accurate. Naturally, I expected all this to be the same with the Babalawos. I was quite surprised when it wasn't general at all; instead it was very specific. A word of caution, don't expect every Babalawo to be accurate or even honest, unfortunately still, there are many in any religion that prey on those who need to hear something. But with me, that wasn't the case.*

I didn't expect to hear what I did, and I really wasn't there for any of this; I was there searching for my cure just to humor my Popi, period. It was explained to me that the 256 paths are roads of the sixteen principle kingdoms; sixteen times sixteen is 256. I learned that Irosun, or Irso, is one of the sixteen principle kingdoms, and that I happened to be the king of this house. "Sure, yeah right, whatever you say," was exactly what I was thinking. We talked about why they were so amused, and I was told that this is the road of the high priest or Babalawo. Not the only one, but the principal road. It was explained to me that while it was a good sign or path, it was also a very dangerous one; those that are born to this path either embrace Orisha worship, or leave it and die young, unless they change their destiny.

Now, I was confused because I thought everyone was born to their path, and while they could influence it, they could not change it. Not exactly, I was informed; in my case IFA, or becoming a Babalawo, was my salvation. Orula or Orunmila the Orisha and patron of Babalawos would save me. Now, I was more confused as I thought becoming a high priest took a long time and much studying. Then it was explained to me that in this sign or road, it is possible and necessary to jump to IFA. Becoming a Babalawo, in effect you skip being a Santero or normal priest of the religion. "Yeah," I thought; "but why would anyone jump when they are already a King?" My surname is King, I liked being a king, and better a king than a peasant I always say.

I must admit when the Babalawos said King, I felt a sense of entitlement. All of the 256 paths, roads, or signs have positive and negative aspects associated with them, at least they are supposed to, as I later learned. I learned that this sign of mine, Irosun Meji was a real stinker. There is almost zero positive about this sign, other than the fact you can change your lot in life by jumping to IFA. I don't want to scare you with a complete recap, and you will have to trust me that not all signs or Odus are like this. Think of it like this: an Odu or sign, path, road, or signal (Odus are called all of these) is our destiny. Just like a roadmap, it is to help show you where the pitfalls are, and how to avoid them. It sometimes makes suggestions that are obvious, and other times the Babalawo interprets the Odu for us, if it isn't simple. Like a doctor, he then prescribes the cure.

Popi and Amado had explained much of this to me beforehand. I listened to my Odu, I kept waiting and waiting for the good to come. The good was that IFA could save me, and actually that was about the only good part. I will share with you some things from my Odu, using mostly my fellow Chicagoan, James J, Kulevich's fine translation from Spanish in his important English book titled The Odu of Lucumi published by Ile Orunmila Communications in 2003.

Irosun Meji is the sign of fire and sight. Mortuary graves were created in this sign, as are accidents, bad luck, and misfortunes. Irosun Meji is the owner of all the holes in the world. IFA says you don't believe in anything and will receive bad news. It is the Odu of theft, trickery, and bad news. Those in this sign are warring, or war is coming. Fire and death are circling your house (literally). One day you have money, the next you do not. Be careful inviting people to your house as they may steal your wife. You have many enemies; the man is being betrayed and deceived. Friends betray you. Watch out for holes. You may go blind. Friends are two-faced and talk behind your back. Suicide and memory loss are possible. The sign represents the sunset, moonless nights, burial, the bottom of the ocean, and the unknown. Someone is tortured in this sign (presumably my brother in 9-11-2001 in the World Trade Center).

Each sign can either be Ire (positive) or come with Ogsobo (negative). There are some positive things that occur in this sign, but precious few. The main point of this sign is to move on or away from it, to be saved by Orunmilla and IFA. Antonio explained all of this to me, and warned me again that people in this sign often abandon Orisha worship and pay the consequences. There is also a famous Pataki (legend) associated with this sign.

My back was still screaming for the promised answer as we concluded the ceremonies. Now it was time to find out what I was here for. Again, Jose sat in front of me and divined for me, this time about my back. After a short time, I learned that the cause of *my pain was indeed witchcraft. I was given the chance to ask two yes or no questions, and I pondered what to ask. I was told to whisper my question into the stone and shell I was holding. It seemed odd to me that Jose didn't wish me to speak my question out loud. My first question was logically if these Babalawos could cure me, or if they had the power to cure me. The answer, fortunately, was yes.*

Basically, this left me with a free question, and I pondered this further. Yeah, I wanted to know who was making this witchcraft on me. I thought and thought, but I certainly couldn't come up with anyone on my own. I was reasonably sure it couldn't be my former wife, as I thought we had settled on good terms. But then I had a flash of thought that maybe it was her Madrina (Godmother), after all, she was a powerful Santera, and maybe she was unhappy that I had divorced my wife. I decided to ask if the witchcraft was coming from my wife or anyone connected with her, the answer was yes.

I was disappointed, but reasoned that it could be her Madrina, or someone else operating without Marjorie's knowledge. Still, I was skeptical and taking all this with a grain of salt, as my back wasn't cured but was still aching. How to cure me was what I wanted to know. This, I learned, would happen the following day. While we ate sandwiches, the youngest Babalawo went to the garden and came back with some nasty-looking green liquid. I was told to drink a large glass of this. It was awful. I was then given a large container of it and told to bathe with it. Amado was to show me how to bathe and I was to drink several more glasses of this before I returned the following day. The cure was to cost another $50.00 and by now I was thinking; why not let them have their fun.

My team arrived at dusk for the cure. Jose was again doing the honors under Popi's watchful eye. Outside to the garden was our first stop, where I drank some liquid under the stars. Into the room we went, and some birds were waved around me and sacrificed. I took a final shower and was told not to dress. Naked, I was led across the street to a walled garden area, petrified I would be seen and giggled at in the busy neighborhood. Apparently, one of the Babalawos had cleared the way as the busy street was now desolate. I was told to face the moon and not to look behind me. Antonio was now speaking African words, and another bird or two were waved around me, and then I heard what seemed to be them being smacked on a rock or the pavement.

Soon, I was handed a linen bundle soaked in blood. I was reminded not to look back. Antonio led me, still naked, to the corner where I was told to leave the bundle in the street and not look back. Next, I was told to hurry back inside and dress. I streaked across the street (OK, I hobbled), and did this happily. "Man, what a bunch of mumbo jumbo, I thought." I asked the Babalawos how the ceremony went and was it successful? They smiled and said it went well and that I was cured. Well, my back didn't feel any better, yet still I thanked them and my team left.

Popi, Amado and I went to Chinatown to celebrate and Popi was positively giddy with the results of my ceremonies. He explained to me that although the sign seemed awful, it was really a blessing provided that I jumped to IFA. We mostly talked about Orisha worship, and he finally left Amado and me to get home as it was getting late for him. Amado and I talked some more, and I asked him about his religion. Amado had never seemed too interested in Orisha worship, although I knew he had been baptized into this religion as a baby.

ANCESTOR NETWORKING

Chapter Four:

We have our one way street and our castle

firmly implanted in our dream world or what some call the astral planes. To expand on the castle a bit, you might like to visualize the lay of the land. Our castles are built like all castles on the highest hill with commanding views so it is easy to defend. In most cases, all the land we can see is the realm of the castle. Like any kingdom there are villages within sight of the castle in all directions. Most of these villagers work the fields, take in the crops and are loyal to the kingdom and more importantly are under the protection of the King (you). Think of the villagers as friends of your ancestors when they were alive or friends of yours who have died. Basically they are people who have an interest in your welfare or are friendly and want you to be safe and succeed. Just like in the waking world there is plenty of information and knowledge to gain. Like in the waking world we have to know where to look and our guides help us here. In the waking world we might use a telephone book to find a doctor, lawyer or accountant; we might see a sign for a pharmacy or grocery store too; but in the dream world there are no phone books or advertisements. There are signs, but until you acquire the knowledge to remember your dreams and interpret the signs these are no help.

When we dream we have five basic types of dreams (not counting erotic dreams). There is the great dream, maybe it is a revelation or inspiration or problem solving dream. Next best is the good dream, perhaps we awake refreshed or are reminded of a pleasant event or it is something that has not yet happened that is positive. The neutral dream is just that neutral. On the negative side for balance (again) we have the unpleasant dream and the nightmare. Why not share another visual for you and your castle. The great dream is a major positive event at the castle big feasts, perhaps a wedding or christening. Maybe your daughter is marrying another princess from a powerful or realm on your border for example.

The good dream: maybe it's the weekend and you are attending Shakespeare's new play or it is a day of family and rest in a lovely climate. The neural dream is a normal workday.

Should the dream be unpleasant chances are some ruffians or thieves are pillaging your outlying villages? The nightmare is when your castle is under attack or siege. Who could be attacking your castle? From within it would be a disgruntled ancestor who is unhappy; like any internal attack it is very important to repair this relationship. Not repairing it or ignoring it could cause a hole in your castle defenses. More likely is it is The Dead attacking your castle from the outside or overrunning your villages. This too needs to be dealt with. You might just send your spiritual guides to deal with this or you might lead them yourself and inspire others to join you. Normally you'd start with your subjects who live in your kingdom to build an army. A king or queen is best served when they know their lands and their peoples; and you can't do this staying behind your walls in the castle.

Naturally all this is pie in the sky until we: 1) Identify our ancestors (a; blood, b; DNA and c; lineage). We should note that while identifying ancestors in each of the three categories, one is sufficient to begin building. Most of us know at least a few blood ancestors and our blood ancestors are a good place to start. 2) Once we have identified one or more ancestor we can begin to build a foundation by improving our relationships with these. How exactly do we build these relationships; well it is easier than you might think.

Many cultures already direct us how to build a relationship with our ancestors and that is a good place to start. In Lucumi like other cultures we have a representation of each ancestor. This can be a simple as a photo or an object they wore like a piece of jewelry or clothing, a brush or even simply their complete name written down and how they are connected to you. In Lucumi and other cultures we have a shrine or throne dedicated to our ancestors. It does not need to be in plain view it can be put away in a drawer or even a closet. A word of caution for those in Lucumi and other African Diaspora based traditions. Your ancestor shrine can be with (part of) either The Dead (los muertos) shrine (boveda) or with your Orishas or separate altogether. However your shrine (boveda) for The Dead should never be with your Orishas.

Now (hopefully) you have your shrine constructed or created what exactly do you do with it? The first thing to remember is you will be using it when you are awake with full control and faculties as opposed to in the dream world or astral planes when you are asleep and in less or have no control. The relation building really is about honoring and including your ancestors in your daily life. Maybe it is every few days or once a week, this is up to you. Have you ever talked aloud to a picture? Asked a dead grandparent for help? Strategized with them? Put flowers on their grave? Left them a fruit or food they enjoyed?

Including them in your life is very much the same, you can have a rigid schedule for it or do it ad hoc, off the cuff. Maybe you say a prayer for them or just say "Hi, I miss you" or ask them for their advice. Like we discussed, it is a one way street and it is unlikely you'll get an answer because: *Your ancestors and The Dead speak to us and advise us in our dreams!* Including them in your conscious state of being awake gives you the opportunity to hear them in your dreams. Of course while you are awake is the easy part that anyone can do.

The tougher part is recognizing and hearing them in your dreams and improving your memory of your dreams, recognizing symbols and how dreams work. To be brutally honest, none of this is very difficult either... if you learn how. This book is designed to give you the tools and knowledge you need to build your foundation. However it is doubtful it will make you an expert any more than reading a how to play tennis book will make you a start winning tournaments immediately without practice.

What would it be worth to you to rekindle and improve your life from the advice and companionship of a dead blood relative? Reconnecting even occasionally with a dead mother, brother, father, sister or grandparent would that have some value? That is a craft that many of us would find invaluable. Yet don't expect to read my book, follow all the steps and become an expert without some serious dedication and perseverance. You did not learn mathematics or grammar in a year did you? Like I said it is a process, for some it is quicker than others. For those who are actively involved in their spirituality it usually goes quicker, if you meditate or practice yoga it helps, really it does. A word of caution to those who study dreams on the Net or social media, I have found almost nothing of value in interpreting dreams there. For instance snow might represent or foreshadow death in a novel or how to book; but it has nothing to do with death from my cheap seats. Nor are most of the symbols so called self-anointed experts claim to be symbols as far as I can tell.

There are things that are of paramount importance though and I'll share a few of them. One is what we have discussed how we segregate the deities, orishas, ancestors and The Dead. Another is their functions and I think I have introduced that. How to build your relationships with them while you are awake is also important and we touched on that. What we have not delved too deeply upon is the actual dreams and how you connect or how you remember and we will soon get to these.

Now that you know who's who, I can tell you that when and if a deity is in your dream it is of maximum importance and yeah this is obvious. For the Lucumi and other African based and Diaspora based traditions reading this obviously when an Orisha is in your dream or a lineage ancestor it is extremely important. We in Lucumi can also utilize the colors, numbers and natural elements of the Orishas and make a correlation when they pop into a dream. For everyone, when we see (or hear) an ancestor in our dreams it is important and we will later help you to focus and remember their role in the dream.

Shall we take a break? I think so, because this is massively important for you to understand, so take a deep breath, because I am going to share and value your dreams during the break. This will help you understand a single dream better and also help you remember better.

Think of each dream as having three parts. The opening scene of a dream's value put at around twenty five percent. The long middle can be a scene of many scenes and this is the least important, it has a value of twenty percent. The final scene of the dream is the third part and it has a whopping value of fifty five percent. It is also the easiest to remember. This valuation is for a dream that does not have an appearance by either God(s) or deity, an Orisha or other immortal (depending on your faith), one of your spiritual guides belonging to The Dead, an ancestor (lineage, blood, or DNA) or a member of The Dead. The rank of importance of these spirits is in the order I just wrote them. We also have dreams with living people and we will discuss these later.

Before we introduce The Dead, we needed to separate A) God or your deities, B) the Orishas or your immortal servants of God such as Jesus, the angels and saints in Christianity, Muhammad in Islam and the Islamic angels (Jibreel, Israfeel, Mikail, Munkar and Nakeer,

Malak Am – Maut, Malik, and Ridwan).
Hinduism might seem a bit more complex, but
really it is not; if we recognize the Devi and
their many avatars these would of course be in
the A) or God section, while devas and
ishvaras might be found in the B) section. It is
really up to you whom you put where
depending on your individual beliefs. If a Hindu
wants to put every deity in A) for example they
can, conversely if they wish to put their
personal devas in B) they can. Understand it is
a flexible category that we are only defining as
a rank. Therefore, whatever your religion is
obviously if God is in our dream, we pay
special attention.

The same is true in other Indian religions,
Shinto, Chinese folk, indigenous, Voodoo or
other African, Buddhism etc. Our focus is less
on A and B and more on C and D. C) is our
ancestors and D) is The Dead. We have
already introduced C) Our ancestors and the
three types of ancestors in the first half of this

chapter.

There is something we should be clear on, I'm trying to not exclude you whatever your faith is, if you're independent, outside of organized religion, don't believe in a supreme being or are not spiritual at all there is benefit for you. This book is I've said is a beginning not an end, a primer or introduction not a oracle for every question. I could have made this book more, but I think "less is more" provided you know how to use the material. There is plenty of flexibility here and you should embrace that and utilize it into your own system. Perhaps you only wish to explore your blood ancestors, you can. Perhaps you want to eliminate something, you can. My choice was to present something massive or something introductory, I choose the latter.

There is a complexity within the ancestors for example, the blood ancestors are easy to understand and the best place to start.

In fact you can eliminate DNA and Lineage ancestors if you like, however doing this limits your capacity too, yet certainly there is significant value in just the blood ancestor connection. It is more important to build the relationship patiently than to try and expand it, like I said it could work in months for you, or it may take longer, but it is worth it and your blood ancestors cost you exactly zero to build except a bit of time.

The next chapter will be a second chapter from my book *Nature's Ancient Religion: Orisha Worship and IFA*. After that we will get back to the nuts and bolts of this book. I'll share a chapter on The Dead, one on The Ancestors, another on Nature and its importance, a chapter on dreams and a final chapter.

Chapter Five

Chapter Eight (From Nature's

Ancient Religion)

Dreaming with Orula

I went to bed late, after talking with Amado and Yoshi in the streaming moonlight reflecting off the river. I was tired and it had been a long day. I normally dream and remember them. Dreaming is something we all do, but not everyone remembers their dreams. I'm normally on the slow side when I awake groggy, and it takes me a while to be alert. Yet I awoke with a start, fully alert, and sat bolt upright. I could feel the blood rushing in my brain, and I remembered my dream with such clarity, it surprised me. My normal habit with dreams is I remember parts, and then I probe those parts and remember more, but this dream I remembered clearly, from start to finish.

Orula (Orunmila) the Orisha of Divination
and the patron of Babalawos had come to me
in my dream. Now, keep in mind I hardly knew
who Orula was at this point. He had never
been in a dream of mine before, and he hasn't
been in one since. I guess he made his point,
and believe me, I was paying attention. It was
a handsome face, with a full head of hair, that
spoke to me, I remember his eyebrows were
very full and bushy, and his black and gray
hair was to his shoulders, naturally curly. His
face had a calm aspect to it, like he was at
peace, yet with a confidence that demanded
respect. In his hand was a staff, around his
neck was a simple yet elegant scarf that
shimmered.

The first words out of his mouth were,
"Hello, Spencer, I am Orunmilla." I wasn't
afraid, there was nothing to be afraid of. I
think I said hello, but I'm not sure; it was a
conversation, although it was really one-sided.

I was mostly listening, in fact I became focused and the rest of the scene that was outside in what looked to be a park during Autumn faded, until he and I were alone, face to face. It was a friendly chat, his words weren't demanding, they seemed to be the voice of reason. His voice was soft yet strong and clear, almost inviting. His next words were, "I have come to you because I want you to help me." I nodded but kept my eyes firmly fixed on his. Then he gave me a history of creation, and told me how pleased he was that I had found Orisha worship. He was serious, but not without humor, and he made some humor throughout the history, and this made me even more comfortable. I felt like a child listening to an elder; he seemed omnipotent, all knowing and all good.

He told me of the history of our religion and then he dropped the bombshell. It really wasn't a bombshell. I know as a student of religion that each religion suffers from abuse. Orunmila explained that our religion was a road, and like any road, some people looked for a shortcut or get lost along the way. He went on to explain how some wayward souls were getting fat from our religion, while promoting fraud. He explained that as with all religions, ours had people using the religion to get financially ahead. Orunmila said there were some who were outright frauds, but mostly it was followers who were being misguided. Some, he said, had compromised our religion and beliefs for the sake of personal gain. Often, this meant telling people what they wanted to hear instead of what they needed to hear: the truth.

Orunmila said that I would learn how easy it was in our religion to find the answers when I became a Babalawo. He then informed me that the vast majority of Babalawos focus is divination, showing followers the way to their respective roads. This, he explained, was the meat and potatoes. He stated that occasionally, the Babalawo would act as a judge or final word when there was a difference of opinion between Santeros and Santeras, but he said this was much less common than divination. After what seemed like hours, he came back to the subject of me. Orula again asked for my help. I remember asking what I could do. He said that he had a specific road for me, little traveled yet important. He said he wanted me to help get people on the right road, no more, no less.

I tried to explain that even if I passed the Babalawo ceremony, who would listen to a junior Babalawo? Rank, after all, was an important part of our religion. He informed me that I had misunderstood. He didn't want me to reeducate or guide those already on the road; he wanted me to use my best efforts with those that were looking for the road, in other words those entering our faith. This, of course, was something that made more sense to me. He told me that this was to be my main focus, my bread and butter. I told him I was worried that I wouldn't find the right people to instruct me, and I reminded him about my recent problems with Antonio. He stopped me mid-sentence and reminded me that he knew all this, and this was a lesson for me. He continued assuring me and actually chuckled knowingly, saying he would put the right persons in my road to guide me, and I shouldn't worry about this. Here I was, still a bit reticent, but I didn't press him on how or who. He just told me I would know them when I met them. It was unusual as he kept telling me all through the conversation to use my mind. "Use your head!" he would say. "Trust your instincts." "I am here to help you." Normally, I am very skeptical, but somehow I knew he would.

I asked him how I would educate the new people, again he told me to, "Use my head." Next, he told me about my secondary task, this he said was similar to the first, but different, he told me to expose fraud and scams when I recognized them, and again he told me he would help me with this. At that time, I didn't know how he would help, but I felt sure that he would. Orunmila told me that my road wouldn't be easy, but if I had faith in him and our faith, he would reward me. I tried to explain I didn't seek a reward. He told me that rewards come in all shapes, sizes, and weights. Rewards aren't just monetary was what I assumed him to mean. He told me that while this would be my road, I would also study the traditional divination forms. He mentioned that I had a special relationship with him and Olofi, and they would both be guiding me. I asked him what if I failed. He laughed and told me I wouldn't fail. Orula added that I shouldn't think I was the only one on this road, he told me there were others. He said he was angry with the outright frauds, and disappointed with those who compromised their beliefs for personal gain. When he spoke of his anger, I could see his eyes change. It was just a flash, but I knew how serious he had become, and I felt a momentary fear for those who would feel his wrath.

I awoke as I said, like I had just ended my conversation, I was 100% alert and remember taking a deep breath as I sat bolt upright from the mat I was sleeping on. I felt like someone who had been knocked out, how they take that first deep breath. It was like no dream I have ever had before or since. It was so clear, even almost a year later, it has stayed with me, embedded in the front above anything else. I can remember every part of the dream clearly, and where other dreams leave after a few hours or a day, this one stays with me. It is almost as if it is prodding me to action.

I talked to Amado over breakfast, and he was somewhat skeptical, who could blame him? We continued with my ceremonies, and an hour later, the house had a visitor. I was sequestered in my room, but I heard a new voice. Shortly, a small man came into the *room and introduced himself as Lazaro. He immediately went to the large shrine or altar of Oshun the river deity to pay his respects. He prayed for a moment, saluting her. Then Lazaro noticed my Opon IFA and Agere IFA and I saw him reel in surprise. The owner of the house came in and introduced me to Lazaro, and I learned he was a Babalawo. He asked me if he might look at the items closer. I said, "Claro," meaning "of course".*

When I returned home in January, I had begun to research not only the religion, but also the religions objects used in Orisha worships. Because of the life force or "Ashe", I had assumed that the older the object, the more Ashe it might have. These objects I was lucky to purchase from a professor of Anthropology, African Art, and Appraisals at the prestigious New York University, Rod Rogers. This fellow had been collecting for fifty years, and as he was retiring, I happened upon a small part of his collection on eBay. The result was I picked up the wooden Opon IFA that Babalawos use to communicate with Orunmila, and the tapper or IRO IFA and the sculptured bowl that holds the sacred palm nuts used to divine, called an Agere IFA.

I watched the reverence and wonderment on Lazaro's face as he handled the African artifacts that were well over 150 years old. He wanted to know how I had come by these, and I explained. He told me that he was an anthropologist as well as a Babalawo, and in fact worked in the branch of the Cuban Ministry of Culture that was anthropological, specifically in the African studies section, and even more specifically in the subsector dealing with my new faith of Orisha worship.

I asked him what the purpose of his visit was. He told me that the Madrina or Santera that owned the house was a friend, and he stopped by on an unrelated matter, and was surprised there was a ceremony going on.

Being the skeptic I am, I excused myself and went and asked Amado and Yoshi if they had told anyone of my dream. They looked me in the eye and told me they hadn't. I went back into the room and Lazaro was still there ogling over the artifacts. I decided to tell him about my dream.

I could see the amazement on his face as I explained. He told me that in his eighteen years of IFA, he had never had a dream with Orunmila, and said it was almost unheard of for a newbie like me. He could see I was dead serious and we talked more about how Orisha worship had found me. I could tell he was keenly interested, but also shocked as my story unfolded. I told him about Antonio and how disappointed Popi was when Antonio had jacked the price up. I explained we were looking for a group of Babalawos that were the real deal, and for a fair price. Lazaro now looked even more perplexed if that was possible. I saw his face in complete bewilderment. And he took a long pause and held his hand out for me to be quiet while he was considering something. He then took out a small Opele, (a portable divination device) and threw it a few times as I watched, puzzled.

Lazaro began by telling me about another part of his life, and now I was the one with the bewildered look on my face. Lazaro was not only a Babalawo; he informed me he was a leader of a group of Babalawos. His group was part of the most important group that makes the Letra Del Ano for Orisha worship. Every year, the Cuban Babalawos get together at the end of the year and make a forecast using their divination skills for the New Year. It is a big deal; this letter has more clout than any other, including Africa. Lazaro and his group within the group are very well respected, as I would learn later. I had read and heard about the letter from Popi and even Amado, and this was impressive. Lazaro explained to me that his group was made up mostly of scholars of the religion, anthropologists, important musicians who play the African drums, and sing to the rhythms of the Orishas, and various other notables as well.

I learned that Lazaro was the chanter or the singer for the Letra del Ano, and had been in this lofty position for several years. His group was made up of about 50 Babalawos, and lesser ranks numbering about 400 in his inner circle or family. He patiently explained that he was a Babalawo who has the highest order possible called, "the secrets of Olofi". Yeah, my eyes were getting wider and wider. Suddenly, I knew what he already seemed to know, and why Orunmila had laughed when I asked how I would find the right path. Orunmila had told me while laughing that he would put the right person in my path. Little did I expect it would be the very next day! My skepticism was almost all gone and I decided to simply go directly to the point. This is something we Americans have a hard time with, yet the

Cubans do so easily. I asked Lazaro if he would consider taking me into his group and performing my initiation ceremony with him.

This isn't a small thing. I told him I didn't expect him to be my Godfather, and he stopped me and said to listen. He said that my story had been so unusual that he had consulted his Opele and that Orunmila wanted him to be my Godfather. He said that this was bizarre because in his eighteen years of IFA, he had only taken two godsons. He explained that his focus was more on studying the religion rather than having a big family. Having godchildren is profitable and rewarding, but it is also a huge responsibility to educate them. This was music to my ears. The more godchildren a Babalawo has, the greater the profit for him, as it is like a pyramid. Each godchild eventually brings people to him, and he profits from these people as well. Lazaro obviously wasn't interested in profit with only two godsons in IFA in his eighteen years.

Everything was going so well, I was expecting the bomb to drop when we came to the price. Yet that was also very fair; 3,300.00 CUC. Perhaps Orula told him to throw me a low number, because this isn't the price Lazaro would charge for a tourist. I have already explained the price structure, and as I said, anything less than 4,000 CUC was a heck of a good deal. This included seven days and sixteen Babalawos, from one of the top groups in the world. Food and drink for all, animals, transportation, the house, yeah it was a great price. Something you should know about me is I don't easily reach into my pocket. I can't remember ever meeting someone out of the blue and plumping down a 1500.00 CUC deposit, and I did not, but I did send Amado to the bank with the magic card. I knew Lazaro had to purchase many things for this ceremony, and especially if I was going to begin soon.

In less than an hour, we had met and solved my problem. Lazaro and I began laughing when I related how Orunmila had laughed when I asked him how I would know the right person. As my new Padrino, Lazaro didn't seem as surprised as me though, he had probably seen many such occurrences in his eighteen years in IFA. I imagine he is used to seeing people like me have Orisha worship find them and IFA, but for me, it was a day I will never forget.

Before when I called Amado in and told him the news and sent him to the bank, I had laughed in and tell him the news, and I laughed openly as I saw his eyes widen and look in amazement. He had never met Lazaro before, yet I later learned Yoshi's stepfather was in Lazaro's group. Yoshi's mother was friends with the Madrina of the house, and that is how we found the house on the river. But if you are thinking Yoshi could have arranged all of this in an hour, you don't know Cuba. Fidel would have a hard time arranging this in an hour in Havana with his motorcade.

Amado was very anxious to tell Popi of this amazing set of circumstances, and so was I. I had asked Lazaro if Popi could be my other godfather, and he said, "Of course." Roberto the Oba arrived, and we began the final day's ceremonies and consultations, where the new Orishas I had washed gave me their sage advice. All and all these went very well and I completed this step. Let's get back to the river for a moment. I'm not a Greenpeace type or an environmentalist activist, but I sure am anti-litter and while I don't use hybrid cars or solar panels yet, I'm cognizant and sympathetic.

Sure, it wasn't my place to be lecturing elders, so I would say I was more pleading with them. I first explained that our religion was the "greenest" of all religions, as our Orishas each rule our Earth's elements. I said that my mother Oshun was the river, and we were making her angry and not respecting her by littering in her waters. I explained that while an Ebbo (remedy) might call for an animal, bird, or plant to be deposited in a river or even the ocean, that should not include the plastic bag. I explained that the bag should be separated as there was nothing natural about the container. I encouraged everyone to spread the word of Nature. Furthermore, I suggested that Ebbos would most likely not work if the Orishas were unhappy.

Logically in my mind, the Ebbo wouldn't work and this isn't an empty threat. If followers are littering the forest, river, or ocean with unnatural things like plastic, surely this doesn't make the Orisha happy, and therefore it is questionable whether the Ebbo gets to where it is going to do its healing if the Orisha is being insulted rather than appeased! Eleggua would not like litter in his crossroads or street corners. Be it Oshun in the river, or Yemaya and Olokum in the ocean, etc. It just seemed incredible that Cubans hadn't seen this before. Now, this is one of my campaigns that I patiently explain every chance I get. Indeed, you have heard it once before already, yet here in greater detail! It is a movement that I feel is important not just for our faith, but for the environment as well. I encourage anyone reading this either in our faith or out of it to consider what I have said, and spread the word, as well as do the right thing when prescribing an Ebbo.

At some point, I would like to get the Cuban government involved in this project to clean up at least their waterways. When I was a boy, I lived on a river that was suffering a similar fate of neglect, and it was the youth that began the basic cleaning. I feel this is a great school project on all levels. It is the kind of project that very quickly brings huge dividends; you see the results immediately. It instills a sense of community pride and togetherness. I am sure the Cubans would embrace these goals, just as many other cultures and nations have embraced them. Furthermore, I think it might be a great project for visiting workers as well. There is now certain and growing amounts of environmentalist tourism, and this would be a perfect project for groups to help with.

I finished the ceremonies and returned to the comfort of my own house, feeling very positive about my first contribution to our faith. I felt that my mother Oshun and my father Aggayu were pleased with me. How could they not be? Cleaning up the environment is a very positive thing. In fact, I felt that all the Orishas were smiling today, some entered into my dreams that night, but not in the same way as my dream with Orula. I awoke feeling refreshed and content. By completing these ceremonies, I was now formally an Orisha follower. Technically, I'm not sure if I was a Santero or just kind of in limbo until I began my Babalawo ceremonies. I should and will find this out on my next trip, because I'm also interested what would have happened if I had failed my Babalawo tests. Where would I have been ranked then? I didn't ask then, and it is only now as I am writing this that the thought has occurred to me.

I learned later in the day that Lazaro had scheduled my ceremony to commence in five days time. I had a bit of a vacation. I had dinner with Popi, Amado, and Yoshi that night; We went out for a bit of a celebration. We chose Restaurant Hanoi, a popular Vietnamese restaurant in Old Havana, near the Capital. We had been going to Hanoi for years, and were greeted as old friends. The food is very reasonably priced, and quite tasty. It is a modest restaurant where mostly Cubans go. It is a wild design with its center being an open air, vine-covered arbor. As it was a nice evening, we dined in the arbor on mostly chicken and pork. They normally have Coca Cola and that was my drink of choice. Popi was *oozing pride that night as not only had I completed this step, but Amado had also renewed his interest in the faith that was so much a part of Popi's life. We made merry for a few hours, and I crawled into bed and awoke to Rosa and Betti pounding on the door the next morning.*

I had breakfast with Rosa and Betti, and then Betti pounded on my back for a couple of hours. I decided that today I was off to one of my favorite locations: The Havana Golf Club. It was Saturday and I knew that many of my friends would be out in force at the golf course. Breakfast for Cubans is a little different than my usual fare. If you are eating in a hotel, you will find the usual fare on the buffet table. Here, it is a combination between an American breakfast and a European one, more meat than Americans use as a rule. At my house, breakfast varies; if I'm having guests, I normally take the reins from Rosa and do the cooking. My breakfast includes some items that are hard to get for the Cubans, and this make my breakfasts a treat for them. I always have fresh squeezed orange juice at my house. Oranges are bought by the sack; a sack is about 120 oranges. The Cuban oranges aren't artificially colored and thus are ripe when they are a greenish color, as opposed to our bright orange Sunkist ones. If the season is right, I also have grapefruit. The Cuban grapefruit is magnificent, but hard to find as much is exported. Guavas are the same; harder to find, but superb.

I have turned the Cubans on to pancakes and French toast. These are the staples of my breakfast for guests. In the Miramar / Playa section of Havana, a new store opened up a few years ago called Palco. Palco has a lot of luxury goods for the diplomatic crowd, and rich Cubans also shop there. It still is a far cry from a top American or European supermarket, but it has some things I find essential. One of these is pancake mix and syrup. Strawberries and jams as well. Shopping is far from one stop in Havana. I usually hit Palco and the Marina Hemingway mini-market, and the old diplomatic store at Aveneda 70. This is another good resource, where some hard-to-find things can usually be found . The Marina caters to the visiting yachts, and thus attracts a well-heeled crowd that has money. You need pockets of cash or a magic card, as the prices run several times our prices in these stores. Not everything is doubled or tripled, but expect to pay 7.00 CUC for a box of cereal, or 6 CUC for imported jam, unless you go for the watery Cuban manufactured brands. Things like laundry detergent of non-Cuban brands sell for 10.00 CUC for a small box. There are still bargains to be had even in these stores if you take the time to look, like artichokes for example. However, these are usually items that aren't staples Cuban diet. These stores (as everywhere) take the magic card or non-American issued credit or debit cards.

.

CHAPTER SIX

The Dead

Now we begin the second part of the book that is less of an overview and more in depth. To help facilitate this each of the next four chapters will be laid out a bit more student friendly. The Dead we can divide into three parts: 1) Speaking to them 2) Receiving messages from them and 3) Spiritual guides.

6.0 Introduction and Review

The Dead we classify as all human spirits who are not your ancestors (Blood, DNA, and Lineage). We send messages TO The Dead when we are conscious (awake); we receive messages FROM The Dead in the sub conscious when we are asleep (dreaming). Indeed it is possible to receive messages from The Dead when we are in a conscious but altered state of mind; yet this is not the focus of this book partially because it is an advanced area of expertise where my skills are limited. Some of the other altered or enhanced states where we can receive messages from The Dead (or ancestors) include (but are not limited to) meditation, yoga, drug induced states (including alcohol), daydreaming, physical trauma, illness, sensory stress or enhancements, sleep deprivation, oxygen deficiencies, fasting, chanting, music, drums, dance, epilepsy autism, psychosis and Nature.

What we call the sub conscious, dream world or astral planes has many names depending on culture and religion; to simplify this we are using a visual aid of a personal kingdom, castle, realm or kingdom outside the castle and beyond the borders of the kingdom. The Dead reside outside your castle walls, the further from your walls the greater chance to encounter The Dead. Some live in your kingdom, these are usually allies particularly in the immediate vicinity of your walls and the term "out of sight- out of mind" seems appropriate here. The further from the walls of your castle the more danger, largely because we encounter Dead who are neutral and those of The Dead who may have animosity toward you, your ancestors or your kingdom. Even within your kingdom there are spies and those with agendas or even those who have given false allegiance to your kingdom. Outside of these infiltrators the only Dead who are (or more correctly should be) inside your castle are your spiritual guides who the Yoruba call egbe. Everyone has one principal guide and two to seven additional guides. Our principal guide is with us twenty four hours each day (asleep or awake) and the others are utilized for tasks as required. We will discuss these more in this chapter.

6.1 First Contact

You remember our castle and the ancestors who live inside the walls. The only members of The Dead who are also inside the walls are your spiritual guides; the other members of The Dead live, work and usually stay outside the walls unless they are attacking and somehow penetrate your castle's defenses. Therefore, logic tells us that your first contact should be with one or more of your spiritual guides. The opportunity is there to receive a reply most nights in your dreams. We will talk more about these guides later in the chapter; the main point here to remember is it is easier to receive a reply inside your castle than outside of it. Sending and receiving messages with your ancestors use exactly the same methodology.

Because first contact with The Dead should be with one of your three to seven spiritual guides who are based inside your castle it make sense to direct your message (think voicemail) to them. Remember too these are independent and loyal spirits; but they are not your slaves. All spirits including even our blood ancestors are under no obligation to serve us, guide us, or speak to us. Just like when we leave a voice message on the telephone, we do not always get a call back. Just like on the telephone if we have a relationship with the person we are leaving the message for, we have a better chance they will return our call. The Dead and our ancestors are the same; if we have a relationship we have built our chances improve for receiving an answer. Look at it like this if I call President Obama, Prime Minister Modi, el chapo, Shakira or a film star like Jet Li unless I have a prior relationship with them it is doubtful they will call back. The same is also true of The Dead and ancestors; we need to remind them how they know us. If I send a message to Bruce Lee, Mandela, Tupac, Jose Marti, Poncho Villa, Xuanzang, Cochise, Mahatma Gandhi or Selena unless I have a relationship or a connection such as they are a blood ancestor; chances are I'll get no reply.

.

6.2 Sending Messages

For the living to send messages or communicate with The Dead the most common (and easiest) way is through speech. The method is similar to when we leave a voice message on a telephone (voicemail). Like the voice message we discussed in the last section there is no way to know if they received it and it is unlikely even if they did that they will respond unless you either have a relationship with them, they are an ancestor (blood, DNA, or lineage), or you can sell or pitch something that may compel them to answer. My opinion is don't waste your energies chasing a dead spirit you have no connection with any more than you chase a celebrity.

Whatever spirit you are hoping to attract I suggest you provide an attractive or compelling environment. Suppose a friend sets you up on a blind date, not only are you on your best behavior but you wanted to meet in an attractive setting right? The Yoruba and Lucumi and other cultures have festivals honoring The Dead, shrines or thrones honoring The Dead and ancestors in their homes or in Nature. Buddhists, Shinto, Native Americans, religions birthed in India and China all share Nature as a central theme. Constructing or having a shrine in Nature has significant benefits we will discuss in a later chapter.

In Lucumi, water is an integral part of a shrine or throne in the home or outside. The Lucumi generally have nine (and sometimes seven) glasses of water on their shrines in the home. Water is much the same as in real life, we offer it to travelers after a journey; a visiting spirt might want a drink! The Lucumi therefore have nine glasses (eight in a circle and one in the middle) on most shrines; we will discuss this more in the next section. The Lucumi are not alone in including water on either a shrine to The Dead or the ancestors, many cultures and forms of spirituality do also.

Other offerings can be food (there are various methods depending on culture how to dispose of the food or how long to leave it out for). A family recipe that was handed down is a great gift to serve. Fruits are a favorite too. Candles are frequently a part of a home shrine; flowers are another staple; some offer spirits items such as wine or rum; a cigar is a staple in Lucumi. Really it can be anything that may be pleasing to the visiting spirit. Now that we have discussed what to offer let's look at the actual shrine and what is included.

Because I have identified two of my guides and my principal guide I have representations of them that are the core of my home shrine. However suppose you don't know your spiritual guides or are just getting started? In this case you make a general shrine honoring The Dead (all). The offerings you share don't change; Great Grandmother's cookies will probably still be a hit! When I started before I identified my spiritual guides I used the nine classes and because I was new, I added the carbonic cross submerged in the center glass as Lucumi suggests. Since then I have largely eliminated Christianity from my personal form of Lucumi and eliminated this, but then when I was new I included it. General shrines can also have a general representation of something representing all The Dead. But the easiest solution for you is to combine your ancestor shrine with your shrine for The Dead. This is very standard for anyone new and in fact many advanced students and followers keep the ancestors and The Dead together. I separated mine many years ago and included my ancestors on my shrine (throne) honoring my beloved Orishas. The Dead however cannot be with the Orishas, they must be separate. We'll discuss the ancestor shrine in the ancestor chapter and more about combining.

My representations on my shrine for The Dead include five objects. The first is my 24/7, or principal ancestor; for him I have a helmet or wooden mask called a gelede. The gelede is Benin in origin (the country next to Nigeria) and about three hundred years old. It is quite handsome and obviously an antique. My second representation is a bronze cast Hindu Brahman princess, she is in a yoga position. Adorning her I have two sets of Hindu beads, one is a beautiful rudrakaha that my great friend Mrs. Indu Ram gave me. The second set of beads is Brahmin and was given to me by Indu's husband. My third spiritual guide is a Druid and he is represented by an ancient shillelagh and some dried berries from a rowan tree. The rowan and all trees have a special significance with the druids and the Lucumi. Personally, I feel strongly that Nature is always represented on any shrine. The gelede is made from a Iroko tree, the rudrakaha are made from the berries of a sacred Hindu tree.

The fourth representation is a special cane made from a special tree in Cuba that is consecrated for The Dead specifically and used by priests of Orun of who I am one. Orun has several mysteries and one is he is the leader of

The Dead. Wrapped around the cane I have a set Orun's black beads. My fifth representation is a simple Yoruba carved antique box from Nigeria, it serves as a representation for all the rest of The Dead who are not my spiritual guides. I keep my shrine for The Dead on a small dresser in my home office and library, where I spend most of my time. Many practitioners suggest a separate room from the Orishas, but I keep my Orishas and ancestors together on another wall in the large room I use for my office.

Now that I've shared the lay of the land we should discuss how the messages are sent. Some practitioners use notes, I don't; I simply talk with each and sometimes together. I greet them when I come in, share with them a problem verbally; sometimes touching the object; but not always. I keep them in the loop, because they are an important part of my existence (as I see it). I might say something like "I sure could use some help with (any subject), or I'd like some advice. Where it gets tricky with The Dead, and our spiritual guides is they often act on their own and this is a lesson we learn. All spirits are like this and often the wise in effect rein them in or are careful what we ask for. Thus, it is better to be specific than general.

Let me give you an example of this. My team is very strong, because I have developed them to be and our relationship is advanced. I spend most days and evenings with them and they are in tune with me and what is going on in my life. I had a fellow taking care of my dad who robbed many valuable items from us. Within a week of discovering this the thief was in the hospital and died days later; coincidence maybe. But it happened again with another person who robbed me, a few weeks later he was dead. I was at a restaurant I used to frequent and they screwed me on a check, it is a big chain in Mexico with two locations in my city. The location I was at was in the center of town, yet a couple of weeks later it closed mysteriously and I learned at the other location the person who screwed me was fired. Another business that took advantage of me burned down the next day. Sure these might be coincidences, but it is not just these examples, I have many. Build your relationship with your ancestors and The Dead they will protect you; but the wise are careful to be specific. Here I used some negatives as examples, but there are many positives I could share with you as well; balance is always looming. The primary theme of this section is we send messages when we are conscious or awake.

6.3 For my Lucumi Friends

The Lucumi have a bit more complex system and for that complexity there are significant rewards. For those of you who are not Lucumi or another West African tradition you can skip this section. Why am I suggesting you skip this section? Because I am going to use Lucumi and Yoruba concepts and words that we do not have the space to discuss in this book. Those outside or unfamiliar with Lucumi are not going to lose anything. If you happen to be Latino, African or Catholic you might want to skim it or read along.

The nine glasses are obviously for Oya and I always supposed the submerged cross is for Aggayu in his role as the boatman in Santeria. Children of Obatala may wish to use rainwater or snow water as those are his natural elements. Oshun's children may wish to use river water, Okie's lake water, Yemaya's and Olokun's seawater (but I would still have some drinking water if I were you). For Awo, I think this aspect of Orun (leader of The Dead) is under taught and underutilized but as I mentioned it is a process to gain the knowledge I'm discussing in the book. Santeria children of Oya should be particularly keen on this methodology and have an advantage like Awo who are Orun priests, A cieba staff may be a good idea or iroko of you are in Yoruba Land. Because of Caribbean, Central and North or South American climates again I can't stress enough the benefits of an outside shrine; the same is true in Yoruba Land. We will discuss this more in a later chapter. Finally, just a quick note on your ide and necklaces for your consideration I have to offer. This probably won't make me many friends with the beaders but I think it is something to consider. Plastic beads are not natural; they are plastic and are sure not ancient. I am surprised so few are making ide and necklaces out of a natural material and painting them the appropriate colors.

6.4 Spiritual Guides

We discussed spiritual guides a bit so far but

we need to expand on them. They are certainly not exclusive to the Yoruba or Lucumi. Some indigenous peoples use specific birds for instance, Christians use angels and saints, many cultures use natural elements, spiritual gurus with many Indian traditions appear in dreams. Ibn Sirin and his students have some useful information, Buddhist rinpoche speak of personal deities who reside on one's shoulders too. Discounting our dreams is not a wise choice. There is so much we do not know and I am still a student. Like many I am learning, investigating, testing and occasionally I find something of value. For me, it takes little time or effort and the price is right! My beloved Lucumi and Yoruba do not put the time in as they should in ancestor and The Dead worship and studies; it is a bit like chanting, we seem to be falling behind the Indian cultures and we should not be.

One great attribute of Lucumi is that finding our spiritual guides is not very complex or expensive as I mentioned earlier. The common problem with anything related to the metaphysical and astral planes is there are many hoaxes, frauds and abusers. These prey on the weak and eager. The main principle in Lucumi and egbe in traditional Nigerian culture is mounting or possession. While the Yoruba in Yoruba Land identify their guides through a ceremony called egbe, we Lucumi have a different process and unlike the egbe ceremony it is free. Science does not help us here as there simply is little (if any) proof to substantiate this occurrence. The concept is simple though and almost every culture as we discussed recognizes it. The concept is that a spirit, avatar, deva or guide takes possession of a human. It is really an amazing experience to watch; for example I have seen a Cuban guzzle two full bottles of rum when mounted and then be more than articulate in his message over the next two hours. There were no tricks like a hole in his stomach or diluted rum either.

Other cultures have various methods to identify a guide and we discussed them earlier. I like the Cuban Lucumi method because it has worked well for me. I mentioned the two main methods of the misa and the tambor earlier and I also mentioned a third method through our dreams. To be able to discover a spiritual guide through a dream is more complex, but not impossible. The main challenge is improving your memory sufficiently to recognize and remember who you were dreaming with. We'll discuss this later in another chapter.

The Lucumi teach that everyone has a principal spiritual guide and he or she is different than the other three to seven. The three to seven spiritual guides we need to inform, plead, ask, and connect with, much the same as another human. Of course we do this in the conscious or while we are awake and alert. If we do not tell them (like your best friend) they do not know; because remember they were humans too and are limited. The principal guide is different in that he (or she) walks beside you 24 hours a day whether we are asleep or awake; the principal does not rest or sleep, they witness everything. Interestingly unlike a friend or one of the three to seven spiritual guides we can't frame what we tell the principal guide, because he or she sees all.

The principal guide also interacts with our three to seven spiritual guides and therefore makes it difficult to lie or spin a situation to the others for us. The principal 24/7 guide sees all you do and knows our weaknesses and strengths. Like one of our ancestors the principal wants us to succeed. I don't exactly know how the principal avoids forming opinions or judging, but they seem to have this ability. I think of it somewhat like each day we get a clean slate with them. However, do not make the mistake of thinking that this means no one is making a tally of our good and bad actions. In Lucumi there are two components who do, the first is our ori that nothing escapes, the second is the Orisha Esu who sees all and reports all to Olorun when he and Iku (the Orisha of death) take our ori to face Olorun after the human shell expires (death).

There is a more complex relationship with The Dead that we will discuss in the chapter on dreams. For the beginner it is of paramount importance to build a relationship first with your spiritual guides and know that once this relationship is built and cultivated other more advanced possibilities exist.

6.7: Receiving Messages

This part of the chapter will seem to some to be the most important part of the book. I want to reinforce that I do not have all the answers. However, I do have enough answers to help each of you begin the process and search for solutions on your own. It was important for you to understand the Lucumi a little before we reached this point. It makes it easier to explain for me and should make it easier for you to understand.

We have established the visualization of the dream world or astral planes for you with the castle. We have also described the inhabitants of the castle are our ancestors and spiritual guides. We have tried to provide you with a visualization of the lay of the land, what you can see from your castle and how your own realm looks, even past what we can see. We have explained the difference between the subconscious dream world and the waking or conscious world. You have learned some of how to and why we send messages in the conscious world and some of the benefits of building your relationships with your ancestors and The Dead.

Conscious vs subconscious it's that simple, we send messages when we are in a conscious state of mind and we receive messages when we are in a subconscious state of mind. Once we grasp this concept we can move forward. Before we attack the dream segment let's discuss a few other avenues to receive messages. Permit me to also state clearly that I am no expert in these, for me it is dreams where my knowledge is based. However I would be remiss if I did not mention at least a few of the other possibilities. Each of these has experts who are worth listening to, and I hope they read this book so we can perhaps compare our research and improve the connection for more. All of these other methods are what experts call "altered states". I think of these as not always pure subconscious, but sometimes on the edge of consciousness.

Some people call these altered states heightened states and I frankly do not know which is better or more accurate, so let's use both. I break these down into two categories: Learned and situational. Let's discuss the learned first because these are more controllable and safer to one's health than situational. Probably the most common of these is meditation; however not any meditation, but manipulative. Like all the learned heightened states (more correct using heightened than altered with the learned states) this is something students work to advance to. Sure it is possible some gifted student achieves this plane of learning with less experience, work and guidance, but that is rare. More common is a student reaching this heightened plane after much education, practice, guidance etc. Things like astral projection or transcendental meditation would be examples of a learned manipulative state or plane. Remember this is not my method, but if you are a student of meditation ask some gurus and I think there is a very strong possibility they can help you receive the messages we are discussing.

Buddhist chanting would be another discipline that I recognize, but am not qualified to speak to. Again ask some gifted priests and I think they will agree this is an avenue that can be used as well. Remember the whirling Dervish? This is an example of how dance can also get you there. Trance music may be similar, I am not sure. Yoga is another well-established learned state or plane, I am confident that some gurus have explored higher or heightened planes of consciousness. I am also confident that should my research be shared with the experts of Yoga, strides can be made. Channeling and Chakra experts too would logically have an avenue. I like to think of all of these I've mentioned as having an advantage and advanced students and teachers having a better chance or a more controlled avenue to success.

Not surprisingly Nature seems to have its own unique connection. Healers who practice and are successful at transferring natural energy logically have an advantage in a successful connection. Massage experts too as well as those practicing Chinese medicine and practices like acupuncture may be able to build a connection. Shaman and indigenous medicine men and women have advantages they can explore. These are all learned disciplines
and in my opinion preferred.

Moving on to our situational altered states, first let me say these are not recommended, they are difficult to control (or regulate) and in fact dangerous. Before we explore these it is also noteworthy to mention that many of these induced methods of altered states affect the memory and recall so chances are you may not remember any messages you receive and this

is why the learned states are greatly preferred.
Let us start with a few with indigenous
histories like sweat lodges and peyote, both
are dangerous and situational, yet both can
produce an altered state. Sleep deprivation,
LSD, certain mushrooms, sniffing glue, opium,
and plenty of other drugs can produce altered
states too. Poisons, heroin, and even
marijuana can produce an altered state.
Alcohol is a good example because indeed it
can produce an altered state, but it affects the
memory. Pain can also produce an altered
state as can a coma. There are others from
what we ingest or do not (fasting) to oxygen
deprivation; but let's move on because I think
you get the idea.

On the less dangerous side would be
daydreams. This is a complicated altered state
that could be learned or could be situational. I
don't really know of any who actively study
daydreams, but I suppose this might be an

avenue also. I am a bit skeptical of these largely because I am not sure they produce enough of an altered state to make a connection. However we should at least recognize the possibility of an avenue.

Two examples of conscious medical conditions where some might suggest there is a connection are epilepsy and autism. I am not qualified to make a determination, but I do recognize that a possible avenue might exist. For me, the best way to receive messages is inside the dream. Our ancestors and The Dead send us messages inside our dreams. There is no difference in how we receive the messages; we use the exact same methodology whether it is an ancestor or a member of The Dead (spiritual guide) inside our castle. Remember inside the castle the only spirits who should be there are our ancestors (blood, DNA and lineage) and our spiritual guides.

For most of the audience receiving actual

messages inside our castle is enough. Most will be delighted to learn how and that they can receive a message from a dead parent, sibling, ancestor or a friend (through the spiritual guides). Friends are more complex because The Dead are more complex than our ancestors. We will discuss this complexity more in the chapter on dreams.

The other thing I want to be clear on is not all messages we receive we understand. Let me provide you with another visual. Messages can be sent in many languages or a code, receiving a message has little value if we do not understand the language it was sent in or have a key to the code. I continually am advising you the audience that this is a process and that I do not have all the answers. Indeed I have made advancements in my research, but as you are learning there are many pieces that make up our mosaic. Each piece of the mosaic has its own complexity; in a way each is connected, but each requires a process to solve. I can provide you with a map but it is not very detailed. I can suggest a route for you to travel, but I can't provide the vehicle or what powers it, you need to do that yourself.

This section is not complete; we will add more pieces in other chapters. The main theme of this section is we receive messages in the subconscious or while we are asleep or in an altered state unlike when we send messages from the conscious state.

6.9 Inside the dream

My avenue or connection is of course dreams, when we sleep to be precise. We have a whole chapter coming up on this so I will be brief. The main highway is our dreams. Everyone dreams, whatever our culture is or beliefs, we all dream. You do not need to be a yoga expert or experiment with drugs to dream, we all do and this is a fact, not speculation.

CHAPTER SEVEN

ANCESTORS

7.0 Introduction

Throughout the last chapter we discussed

several topics and here we will expand on these. We learned that we send messages to The Dead and ancestors in the conscious and receive messages in the subconscious. We learned that the methodology is the same for sending and receiving within our castles. We discussed that all members of The Dead and ancestors were human and unlike the Orishas or other immortals they cannot be in two places at once, so we must be more persistent and patient.

7.2 Blood ancestors and a twist

Do you remember back when we touched on the subject of ori? Ori is what the Yoruba call soul, but as I said it is a more. Called the divine spirit ori is our center or core, what lives past the current body and in the words of Professor Albus Dumbledore "goes on". I don't mean to make light of ori or whatever your culture or individual set of beliefs calls ori or the soul. Yet the reality is J.K. Rowling who wrote Harry Potter made a very deep concept simple with those two words "goes on". No one knows where "on" is or even if there is an "On". If you're reading this book, chances are you are a believer of "On". I can also swear up and down on a stack of whatever religious text you put in front of me that I have received and do get messages from my ancestors and other immortals in my dreams. However some are not going to believe me.

Others will be open to the possibility and want to learn more. To be honest, this is probably where you'd find me if I was an outsider reading this book. I view myself as logical and cynical as a rule. I don't buy into changes in my philosophy easily and I often use risk vs reward as a way of determination. If I was reading this the first thing I would look at is the reward and I would agree it is substantial. Next I'd look at what does it cost in time and money and I'd determine this was minimal. I would not be overjoyed it is a process with a small chance of immediate success. However to make a small shrine for my ancestors and The Dead and maybe keep it in a drawer, say hello on occasion would not be a sacrifice that I would shy away from. Even if it took five years and I failed to connect it would not cost much and chances are if I did connect it would come much sooner. I'd also like the fact I could learn something about my dreams, and improve my memory of my dreams. For this logical cynic, I'd probably say "why not!"

Then there are those who are searching for a connection and these include the 175 million in my culture in The Diaspora and Yoruba Land and those in other cultures who are active in ancestor veneration. For these my advice is, why not try my method?

Our blood ancestors as we have talked about

are fairly obvious (unless of course you are an orphan). I wish I had some sage advice for my orphan friends, but unfortunately I don't have much. There is also the reality that past a couple of generations (of our four grandparents) it gets murkier. Websites like Ancestor.com sure can help searching records, but unless we get very lucky a five or more generation gap is tough to tap for most of us. With all ancestors it is important to remember the farther they are from us generationally the more descendants they have. Why is this important? It is because fact of the The Dead and our ancestors can only be in one place at one time unlike an immortal, Orisha or deity. Suppose your dead mother had ten kids and they are all living. Just like when she was alive, her attention is not only with you but also your nine siblings. If the same mom had two children then she is obviously going to spend more time with you or be more available to you. Logic tells us if you are from a bigger family, you'll need to be more persistent to get the messages you send through to your ancestor. Logic also tells us that you'll need more patience when receiving messages.

Remember ori (the soul)? Now here is the twist. Our ori can have already had multiple human lives and that means multiple ancestors. If you are African American for example your ori could have had an earlier human life where it was white....GASP! If you are white you could have had a Black ancestor. So the lesson here is to be compassionate of others regardless of their race, because all human hearts are pink and we all bleed red. Is there any way to access our ori ancestors? I have not come across a method yet, but I am still hopeful. There is also a school of thought that our principal guide and the three to seven additional guides in The Dead are actually our ori ancestors. I only learned of this recently, but on the surface it would seem to make sense to me. In any case the ori ancestors with or without the spiritual guides is the twist I spoke about.

7.4 For my Lucumi friends

I want to be a little clearer on how you should be valuing what we collectively call IFA culture. The first thing is valuations are subjective and we start with two branches of the tree who are supposed to work together but often do not, Ifa (Orunmila's priests) and ocha (santeros and santeras). The debate goes something like this: ocha feels it has more value because most priests of Orunmila are also santeros. Orunmila's priests feel that not only do they outrank santeros and santeras, but the education and powers they specialize in are superior. The fact is even the lowest omo awo does outrank all santeros and santeras and those who only have a cofa or a mano de Orula. What an arrogant young omo awo learns is it is very easy for any long tenured elder santeros or santeros to circumvent him. This is a frequent occurrence and soon finds the young omo awo in multiple lectures from his elders on humility and tact.

There are also many exceptions to the idea that Ifa priests have more education. There are many santeros and santeras who are better and more accurate diviners than a full Awo and certainly better diviners than an omo awo who is in training. There are many osianistas who are more gifted in herbs, plants and healing than Awo and even some Awo's who have received Osian as an Ifa power. There are gifted oba who despite being outranked by an awo can be more talented. I always like to point out that while rank determines the last word; elders and tenure are much more respected and loved in the culture whatever side they are from.

Students and elders know that while we receive ashe from a leader on both sides of the aisle and receive a title; this is putting the cart before the horse, because a title has little value without the accompanying training and education. I would love to see us reconstruct the levels of rank and include on the ocha side the osianistas and the oba. I'd like to see an omo santeros/ santeras rung and I would like to see the women who lead the principal houses be above every rank in ocha. On the Ifa side there is the first hand or mano or cofa and I would like to see more education be available to this rank even though it is the lowest and also mostly a simply ceremony. I'd like to see the omo awo having two levels, one for those washing and one greater for those who are already santeros. The same for full Awo's who have completed their basic training and are found qualified to have at least some clients on certain levels. Of course I would like to see the rank of Baba Awo return to a confirmation and the knife be exclusively for a senior Awo has actually earned it.

Which is greater and lesser ocha or Ifa? I would not hazard an opinion because they are both important and give balance to our culture. Only men can reach the highest level of Ifa and only women can reach the highest level of ocha (in Lucumi). This is correct and should not be changed. To return to our topic of our ancestors and The Dead interestingly both fall outside the jurisdiction (and sometimes petty battles of the two). However both ancestors and The Dead are extremely important to both ocha and Ifa. How does one value The Dead, Ancestors, ocha and Ifa? My habit is to value them all equally. I do this because each is a conduit to God (Olodumare, Olorun and Olofin), each has unlimited power and protections that no student or master will ever complete in a lifetime.

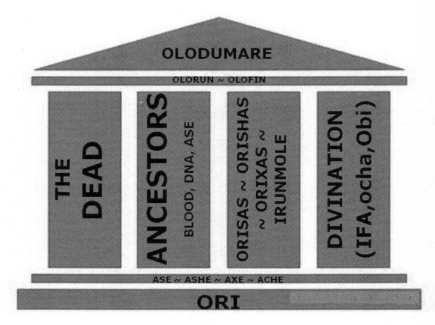

I love the fact that The Dead is free of charge and the blood Ancestors are free of charge (in Lucumi). I like the fact that through the internet we are able to find our DNA ancestors on the internet for around 50.00 USD. One of the things I love about Lucumi is we do not need to pay for an egbe ceremony like the self-named traditionalists do, for us we have free access to learn who our spiritual guides are in The Dead. Unlike Christianity or Islam or many other forms of worship we in

Lucumi have an unlimited source of power and protection that is free for those who study it. If we look at the valuation The Dead would have a valuation of 25% for free! The ancestors 25% are a bit more complex because your lineage ancestors (who are not free) and that we have two sets of (ocha and Ifa) have more value than a DNA ancestor or even a blood ancestors! The reason why is because they have knowledge, they were leaders in our culture and acquired wisdom. If I was making a valuation it would be like this: Blood 5%, DNA 3%, Ocha lineage ancestors 8%, Ifa lineage ancestors 9% (totaling 25%). To go just a bit further with our Orishas 25%, technically this is really 25% + 8% or 32% because the lineage ancestors come from even the lowest rung on the ocha rank (Necklaces). Ifa's 25% is also augmented by the 9% of lineage ancestors that are received in the lowest rung of the Ifa side through the mano or cofa de Orula for 33%. Neither ocha nor Ifa is free, but both also have unlimited power and protections. Blessings to all and ashe! Lucumi Baba Awo, Ogbe Osa, (Charles Spencer King) The Commission # 247, 2015.

7.7 Blood Ancestors

I want to reiterate that just having your Blood Ancestors is enough to make contact. Think of it like this: We have discussed neither our ancestors nor The Dead can be in multiple places at the same time because the spirit was human. Spirits that are from humans and animals have limitations; they do not suddenly get super powers after they die! Obviously the more ancestors we can identify improves our chances of at least getting a message to the ancestor we are targeting to speak with. Of course we all have ancestors from our mother (maternal side) and our (paternal side). Each side should be at least represented on your shrine. If you have multiple representations on each side of your family tree (maternal and paternal) it is at least twice as good and you improve your chances of making one or several connections.

DNA and lineage ancestors simply increase your odds of a connection. Perhaps you do not have the money, opportunity or desire to find out your DNA and/or your lineage ancestors; that is OK, your choice. However, you still can make a connection with your blood ancestors. What I am laying out for you is what worked for me and that was great. For example, it can sometimes take a week for me to connect or be contacted in a dream, but rarely more than that. Some ancestors it can take longer to connect with; others it could be within 24 hours. Indeed, I have a large network that I have built over the last ten years. Maybe I am gifted, maybe you are more gifted or less, I don't know. Not only do I connect faster with certain (as opposed to other) ancestors; but some I connect better with and understand better than others. It is not always the ancestor who I was closest to in their life; often it is another; sometimes even ones I never met in their lifetimes. All of these things you need to work out yourself. I can't make sweeping statements, because I mostly know about my own; and a bit about others I have helped or those who have helped me. Therefore, when I say "I am not an expert" or "I have limited experience", it is not out of humility, it is accurate.

In the upcoming chapter we discuss various contributions Nature can make to further or initiate a connection. The point is that there are many avenues and as we discussed earlier improving an environment can help us develop the connection. Think of it like a friendship or most other types of relationships; it needs time and mutual desire to develop. The first contact can be foreign; this is another reason why it is important to send messages when we are conscious, when we have more control than in the subconscious. Our ancestors are much easier to connect with then The Dead because we have a mutual interest in our lineage, the family, also there is curiosity on both sides. If we are connecting with a member of The Dead that we knew in our lifetime it's also easier to connect with than a complete stranger.

The more inviting we make the environment, just like the more connections we have identified or by using the link with Nature improves our chances of making a connection and developing and improving a relationship. The fact is our advantage is in the conscious world while we are awake, and the wise make the most of it. In the subconscious or dream world the advantage we have in the conscious world is greatly reduced. The understanding I am trying to share is that just like when entering any relationship it is logical to have as many things as possible in your favor. Remember the cookie recipe that was handed down from your great grandmother? Little things like that will help you sell yourself to your ancestors; when we include them in our lives in a practical way we improve our chances to initiate and build a relationship. If you happen to know your grandmother's favorite flowers, pick some for your shrine. My Dad for instance loved fruit pie, dark chocolate and beer. My mom liked cigars, jigsaw puzzles and sourdough bread. My Gran loved playing cards, my brother loved cigars, single malt scotch whiskey and corn. All these help; one of my grandfathers loved to speak Spanish and timepieces. Just like a date or a sale if you know your target's interests, you improve your chances.

Building the relationship with your spiritual guides is also sound strategy, learn what they like and share. In the folowing chapter we will discuss receiving messages in the subconscious. One thing I suggest is in the conscious world while you are awake throughout the process you talk to your ancestors about your frustrations of the process. Tell them the parts that you are challenged by, tell them your successes and failures during the process. If you make them part of your end of the process, perhaps they will make it easier on you, speed up the process for you or throw you some nugget to help. Human nature is that people like to be asked for help, even if they are unable to help; it makes us feel good to be asked.

All of these suggestions you need to give a chance to work, the process is long. However, it is in the end like most things, trial and error. What works for me well, may work for you not as well, or not at all, my keys are different than yours, my ancestors are different than yours. My culture or religion or philosophy might be different than yours; in many ways you must be an investigator, a creator, a facilitator, a salesperson, an analyst or a marketer. If you have an expertise or are a student of meditation, yoga or the many other interests we have already named, cultivate that, use that connection to connect. Don't try one; try many, and keep trying them. When you finally do make a connection, continue to look for and investigate others. Maybe you lose your voice and can't chant, or lose a hand and can't drum, or your strength in Nature is the ocean and you move to the desert for work. Maybe you have a certain bird and they migrate; it is always wise to cultivate other avenues, not have all your eggs in one basket. Use your head, be creative!

7.9 Patience and Me, Myself and I

Suppose you picked up a book on the

subject of exercise or a diet; the book alone will not help you lose weight, it is a process. This is the way to look at this book too; it might seem like I am harping to everyone or making this point endlessly, and I am. Just like a child on a trip you want to know when we will get there. Like a student you start with an education and if you are committed to the education your chances are greater to succeed. Suppose you graduate and desire to be a professional, few immediately start their own firm; most start at an entry level and grow. The Boy Scout earns merit badges; the Girl Scout awards, both are a process.

I understand you wish to see results and know that you are moving forward. I understand your goal is to connect and converse with an ancestor or The Dead. If you study this book you will see progress! You will recognize that you are not only remembering your dreams better, but you are understanding their significance more; not completely, but more. I don't always understand every dream's significance, nor do I remember every dream, because even for me, ten years later it is a process. The yoga student advances but rarely reaches Nirvana, the same with the student of meditation. Enlightenment is elusive, but we grow during the process, we improve during the process. You will grow just as I have during the process; but it is not overnight. How soon before you see results? You should see some almost immediately if you follow the steps and are committed to the process. However that does not mean I can guarantee you will make a connection almost immediately. Making a connection can be a matter of months or years; everyone is different, their commitment levels are different. If the spirit wants to connect with you this is a huge boon. If they don't the process will take longer, you'll have to sell them, entice them and appeal to them.

Some steps will be easier for you than

other steps. This is why I am appealing to your strengths or a multi avenue approach to your education. Perhaps you are not a musician, a poet, a naturalist, or meditate, it is OK, and you do not have to be, in order to be successful. But use the individual strengths you do have, because they may help. Perhaps you are rich, a great cook, feel a spiritual connection, are a dedicated student, these all help, so use them. Study your ancestors just like you would study a customer or a company you wish to get a job from, all this helps. It shows your ancestors you are committed to connecting.

There is an expression "There are no bad students, only bad teachers." I readily apologize for my fireside chat manner; sure maybe an impersonal textbook would be easier for you. The thing is I do not enjoy writing in that style, I like to "connect" with my audience, I like to be available for them. In a way this book is somewhat underground, it is self-published, you might find a grammar mistake or several and I apologize. Maybe this book will find you after I am dead and gone, so we won't get to "connect"... then again maybe you'll connect with me as a member of The Dead and send me a message saying "Your book changed my life" and I might just respond! I enjoy contributing to anyone's spiritual growth and though my contribution may be small, it gives me a purpose, makes me feel good about my work. You might think this book is bullshit or a hodgepodge. But an education is never easy, it has peaks and valleys.

I am not a guru, I am just a fellow traveler or student who is a bit further down the road than you are, so look at me that way. Within my own culture and religion I have a lofty rank; but I am controversial, a maverick, many do not approve of me or my teachings. I do

not seek their approval, accolades or support.
It is not important to me if some conservatives
do not respect me and my progressive
message or even if they do not like me! I do
not enjoy trying to force my opinion on others
any more than I like when they try to force
their opinions or teachings on me. I am
comfortable in my role as a primary teacher; I
do not want to teach experts or advanced
students. I enjoy being a student of many
cultures and spiritualties; I like interacting with
everyone even if they are outside my culture
or religion. I am approachable! I like Nature,
sports, women, art, culture, philosophy,
friendship and many more things besides
dreams and Ancestor networking! I can go for
hours or days without discussing culture or
religion or spend hours or days only discussing
culture or religion. I'm probably a lot like you,
I'm sure you have strengths that I could learn
from too.

Some people find me arrogant or aloof;

they insist I speak about me or I more than we or us. The reality is I am somewhat; despite being approachable, some might say I am quirky. I have a temper like my father, Aggayu, the volcano; I have an ego that sometimes flows like my mother Oshun, the river. I am progressive, but old school, manners are important to me. I am like this book, far from perfect!

ANCESTOR NETWORKING

CHAPTER EIGHT

Dreams and altered states

8.0 Prelude

Let's start with a fairly recent dream of mine for illustration and discussion and then we will continue to some memory aids for you. This dream is from last year; it might surprise you at the clarity in the retelling. It hopefully will show you how when it is an important dream, we can focus and remember clearly, although not as much as an experience in the conscious world when we are awake. Interestingly subconscious experiences can be as profound and clear as conscious memories are; in both cases over time the memory is reduced. I often make the case that a dream can actually be more committed to memory than an experience when we are awake. That might seem like a stretch for most of you at this point in your educations, but let me provide an example. If and when you do reconnect with an ancestor or a member of The Dead you knew personally; would not that be an important memory?

My Dream

The first thing I remembered was that I was shot once in the chest at twenty paces with a medium caliber handgun at a random shooting. I made it to the local hospital when an ambulance drove by and stopped on its way back to the hospital from lunch. There I was successfully patched and in pain. The young Indian doctor informed me the bullet was a nine millimeter that had glanced off a rib and exited my chest cavity. Her brown eyes were truthful when she added that I was lucky. I assumed this was a random shooting and I was simply in the wrong place at the wrong time. After the obligatory police interview the Doc said she was leaving for the weekend with her husband and gave me the choice of spending the night in the hospital or being released. She told me a few members of the press were waiting out front and offered to sneak me out the back, I accepted. Strangely I was invigorated and alert, it seemed to me that Iku (death) had only teased me and this energized me. The alley was well lit with an amber glow as I made my way to find a taxi. A neon light said New York Presbyterian Deliveries.

Unfortunately I discovered my shooting was not random when my attacker stepped out of a doorway with a Smith and Wesson ten millimeter shouting the Takbir, Allahu Akbar! I remembered laughing at the irony and decided no, I'd continue to write about the Islamic terrorism that is invading my world. Shot now with a larger caliber in the leg, groin and chest (twice) my attacker brandished a machete type weapon and approached to take my head. I felt a familiar complete calm despite realizing these bullets had done significant damage. I recognized this calm and accompanying shift to super slow motion, I had experienced it before, although not often. This altered state I recognized from danger and previous life threatening situations. The slow motion also accompanies what the warriors of old call "battle frenzy". I waited patiently for him to approach as I took in the gleam of his weapon. It seemed like ages for him to advance five paces. I noticed we were still alone in the alley and this seemed strange because it is a big hospital and the street a stone throw away was busy in the early evening. It also seemed odd his revolver had only fired four shots; perhaps the last was for him and martyrdom, I seemed to decide.

Feeling less fragile than the feigned look of helplessness I acted, he finally reached me with his raised weapon and I noticed the shift of weight as he prepared his descending blow. The ancient battle frenzy of my ancestors from Wales was upon me as lunged and concentrated an energy blow to his chest. I had caught him off guard; the fool had fallen for the oldest trick in the book. I heard him gasp as my blow landed adroitly to his solar plexus; the machete fell slowly and rang as it clanged on the asphalt settling finally. I could not rise, but I wrestled the pistol out of his head and shot him Moe Green style through the eye. He immediately went listless and something gurgled from his mouth; maybe it was a curse or prayer in his native tongue.

Two young men now appeared at my side and one ran to get help while the other shook at the gory scene. I told him to relax, but a wry smile and one word was all I could manage. The world sped up to normal speed for me and the searing pain made me fight not to pass out or give up. Swooning now images passed quickly as I was losing consciousness. I was not quite out yet, but very close; I was shaking as shock was overtaking me. This time I saw Iku and Esu approaching and this confirmed the end was near; where the Hell was the help? I was at the damn hospital! The warrior who is my 24/ 7 guardian I now saw for the first time, gosh he was tall skinny and jet black. His lance and shield were replete with feathers and design. I heard voices and also my ori (the divine spirit some call soul or atman) I felt detaching, but help had finally arrived. The last thing I remember was focusing on my ide, the bracelet honoring Orunmila that cheats death. Was the help in time? I'll never know as I awoke from this nightmare.

Just so you know, I awoke in a sweat, tears in my eyes, shaking...so much for the cool hero my dream centered on! Now we will analyze my dream: The first relevant point was Orishas Esu and Iku were in the dream making the dream very important. My 24/7 guide was also in the dream. Secondly, I did not die in the dream although I was a whisker away from death. Obviously it was a stern warning, not to be taken lightly and it was a sad dream as I awoke with tears in my eyes. The scene was vivid, even for me with my training, meaning clarity and certainty. Did you remember that the doctor was Indian and female the same as one of my three – seven spiritual guides?

Remember the location, NYC, Manhattan and a city I love. The advice and message though is very clear, I'll never visit Manhattan again, and perhaps that is why I was crying. My only brother was killed on 9 -11 -2001, in the World Trade Center by radical Islamic terrorists. My brother and I connect regularly (usually a couple times a month) in my dreams. New York has always been a special place for me, a positive place; I love the city and her leadership, creativity and energy. Terrorism has made long distance travel a frustration for me (unless you send a plane for me). Maybe I am getting old or set in the pattern, but new experiences that involve distance I am less and less interested in. Still, it is possible because, I never say never.

8.1 Pops

My Dad and I were very tight before he died of Alzheimer's and like my brother Andy, I connect with him at least a couple times a week. You see Andy is busier with his family and large circle of friends and neither can be in two places at once. Pops however has a much smaller circle and this last year has been awesome for me connecting with him. He lived with me since 2001 until he died last year. Most of the time his memory was impaired because he had a subdural hematoma after a bad fall in early 2002 that took him four and a half years to fully recover from; and I helped him rehab from. Then we had a great eighteen months where we did a bunch of traveling and played golf most days. Sadly, he was diagnosed with Alzheimer's in late 2004; oddly he had entirely skipped dementia. We tried all kinds of clinical trials, every drug imaginable and some not readily available in the US, despite some inhibitors there is no cure. Pops being a devout atheist did not stop me from using ever contact and skill I had to extend his life. In fact we did and I believe he has the record for the longest surviving person in the world with the disease full blown (stage 7). He lived twelve years!

The funny part of this and why I am sharing this chapter of my life (that I would not trade a minute of despite his impaired condition) is this: Obviously my ancestors (and his) were and are very pleased with me I made this substantial commitment. However when I first connected with Pops he was full of health and not impaired at all. Along with this joy we talked a lot about the dream world and the ancestors he was now a part of. He filled in many holes for me and early on (I connected with him in about six weeks, largely because he was new to the astral planes and had to learn the ropes, I suppose). But the funny thing was he had asked his trainer if he could be my 24/7 spiritual guide, and was told "no". My father has never taken the word "no" lightly, and apparently he made quite a scene and got into some hot water!

Naturally we receive our 24/7 guide at birth, not in the middle of our lives and there is no changing this guide! These guides like we have discussed are ori ancestors and they earn and train for the position of 24/7 guide. Pops I've since learned was not an old soul like me; he is only a few generations old in terms of ori. Over the last year he has accepted this fact albeit grudgingly and he still whines about it on occasion! I love my Dad and reconnecting with him in the afterlife through my dreams is in a word, awesome!

My mom and I have not been able to connect yet, but I do connect with an ancestor on her side from the 1500's. My dad's father and some Cottle kin I have connected with and we are building a relationship slowly that I am enjoying. Other than my paternal grandfather I have not heard from any other grandparent...yet. Like I said, it is a process. I will tell you though my Cottle named ancestors are very happy I dedicated this book to them! (see dedication).

8.2 Boosting Memory

If we can't remember our dreams, we can't connect with our ancestors or The Dead, it is that simple. If alternatively you are in another altered state you can't connect if you don't remember. When we were young riding a bicycle seemed a daunting task; but soon we were buzzing around the neighborhood. Remembering your dreams is a process that may seem daunting, but it is really not too difficult, if you practice. Progressing in this chapter we will discuss the more complex task of analyzing your dreams; but first you need some aides to help you remember.

Just building your shrine will help; it helps like a sign does for a retail business. Without a sign and a dark window your business would not get much walk in traffic would it? Talking to your ancestors and The Dead on your shrine will also help. Think of this like advertising, the more members on your shrine you have identified the greater the "reach" (to use the advertising term). The more times you talk with these, the greater the "frequency" (to use the advertising term). The first step to remembering your dreams is to keep a journal or pad and pen next to your bed. Dreams evaporate from our memory quickly, so it is of paramount importance to write down all that you remember. This means before you leap out of bed and brush your teeth, before you kiss your wife or say "good morning", immediately. Seconds matter, especially at the beginning of your studies. Alternately you can use a phone to record your voice and later transcribe the dream to your journal.

To begin with, try to focus on only the dream you wake up to. Later you can explore several dreams during the same sleep, but at first limit your attention to the last dream, the one you wake up to. Remember the values of parts of your dreams that I shared with you earlier in the book. Science insists taking a nap or several naps help us remember our dreams. When we make a conscious commitment and frequent reinforcement to remember our dreams, we start to. In some ways our objective is to link the conscious with the subconscious. When we improve focus during the conscious state to memorize our dreams it helps. Some people find adding drawings to your journal helps. Re- reading your growing journal before you go to sleep helps greatly, particularly your last few dreams that you recorded. If you sleep with a spouse or significant other, certainly enlist them to help you. This starts with sharing your project with them, but it is wise to discuss and solicit their help. It can be simply having them be quiet for a few minutes to helping you write down your dream. A supportive partner is essential to this project; a non-supportive partner can and probably will prohibit you from reaching first base.

Like I said it is not complex, it is doable. You want to be persistent, but if for example your children run in and jump on the bed it is not a catastrophe. If you take some days off it is OK; maybe you take the summer off that's fine. However, like a course of study you won't graduate until you finish the work, but you will be learning along the way. One note is alarm clocks are not helpful to remembering your dreams, especially when you need to get up to turn the alarm clock off. If you require an alarm clock, try to start waking five, ten or fifteen minutes before it goes off. Use it as a last resort or a backup. The fact is that your improved focus over the course of this study will quickly allow you to rise before or without an alarm clock, but it is like anything else, it requires practice. If you follow these very simple suggestions you will improve your ability to remember your dreams quickly.

8.3 The Nightmare

We all have woken up from a nightmare, our usual response is we do not want to fall back asleep right away. Since our childhood we have all been challenged how to get rid of a bad dream. Our parents sometimes helped us back to sleep by comforting us, distracting us, or inviting us into their bed to resume sleeping. When we become parents we use these same ancient methods to calm our own children. Now that you are beginning to understand the difference between us controlling the conscious and the subconscious we are trying to understand and ultimately influence, we look at the nightmare differently. It is still unpleasant for us and our loved ones, but we now agree there may be an important message in the nightmare.

We realize now that along with the cures of our parents the main thing about a nightmare is we have been conditioned to forget it as soon as possible. This conscious decision has had farther reaching effects than just the nightmare. Since childhood we have made a conscious effort to forget our dreams. Now when we want to use our subconscious to connect with our ancestors, we still have this substantial conscious barrier to break or circumvent. Yes, it is a process once again. There are two choices here to break or circumvent this habit; the easy one is to continue building and hope you can both forget the occasional nightmare when you wake up and remember the connection dream regularly. Many are successful in this; others are not. How long this takes depends on the individual, for a few it is weeks, some it is months; others it is years or never.

The quicker way to break the barrier is to try and remember your nightmare(s). Add them to your journal too and dissect them. There are a few methods that help induce nightmares or bad dreams. For me personally whenever I eat an apple or two before bedtime I get a nightmare. Sleeping face down helps, vitamin B-6 helps, melatonin some find useful. If you happen to remember a former nightmare you have had, focusing on that before sleep can help. Gore or horror films work for some people too. Once the barrier is broken then remembering the positive and teaching dreams you want to remember comes easier. Of course this is the bolder, more uncomfortable approach, but your ancestors are worth it, right? The bottom line is now you at least understand why it can be difficult to remember our dreams. The habitual conflict of the conscious mind telling us when we are awake to forget the dream must be resolved.

8.5 Symbols

With symbols in our dreams we have some good news and some bad news as the saying goes. The good news is contrary to almost everything you've read in books or online; symbols are very easy to understand! On top of that, I can assure you that all of the basic knowledge you require, I will share with you here in this short section and save you a tremendous amount of wasted time chasing symbols. Therefore let me continue with the good news. We have already identified the symbols that are of massive importance, any of your ancestors, members of The Dead and God and other immortals (like the Orishas). Dream "experts" claim symbols in your dreams are important and they are; but not the symbols these experts sell you. There are many sites on the web that operate like a search engine such as Google; you plug in a word and the site generates what this symbol represents in a dream. This is complete and utter nonsense otherwise known as bullshit. You plug in the word "snow" for instance, it generates "death". The reason this is nonsense is there are NO universal symbols (the exception is for Yoruba cultures we'll discuss later). What is a symbol for me is not a symbol for you; or your symbol is not my symbol. Yep, and this is the bad news; you must record and generate your own list of symbols besides the obvious ancestors, The Dead, God and immortals. This too is a process and obviously it goes in your journal.

Let me give you an example, I have a client whose symbol of importance and truth is the hummingbird. Whenever a hummingbird appears in his dream, the dream comes true. Recognizing the hummingbird has actually saved his life twice. I have dreamt of hummingbirds or had dreams with hummingbirds and no such significance results in it. Native Americans and my Yaqui friends here in Sonora often have birds, jaguars and the blue wolf as being powerful messengers in their dreams. I have another client in India that snakes do the same thing another there it is the tiger, one in China that it is the monkey, another in Jamaica that it is a crab, a Mexican that the manta ray speaks to her, another client in California who it is a giant sequoia tree. The Yoruba and several cultures have trees or the spirits of trees that speak to them.

8.5 Ancestors

Let's have a quick review. There are several types of ancestors, the most common is a blood ancestor and these are also easy to identify (and verify through basic divination such as the obi coconut). They are also very helpful (usually).

We interact with our ancestors (all of them) in the dream world where they and our personal guides guard our castle. Ancestors we do not interact with outside our castle. When we speak with them on our shrines, they do not always get our messages because unlike immortals they can only be in one place at one time. There are also DNA ancestors that are harder (but not impossible) to identify. The Yoruba, other West African traditions and those based in The Diaspora also can earn ashe or lineage ancestors through ceremony. These are well documented and identifiable, very powerful; but also can only be in one place at one time and are in demand. Finally, with this last group and all cultures believing in the soul (going "on") we have ancestors from our ori (soul's) past lives and those related by blood to them. These are the hardest to identify, but possible. Now you might have noticed that as the book progressed I have become more convinced of the guides of The Dead actually being ori ancestors. I have become convinced of this after investigating it while I have been writing and spoken to each of my guides and confirmed it.

My first question was should I move the ori ancestors to my ancestor shrine from their current location on my shrine for The Dead? (Remember mine are separated unlike most priests or members of cultures outside the Lucumi – Yoruba.) The answer was unanimously "No". The reason is these are our connection to other members of The Dead (besides our ancestors). Therefore, our ori ancestors stay on the shrine of The Dead.

Our ancestors are our strongest allies, our inner circle and once we build a strong relationship with an ancestor they will often act on our behalf with little or no coaxing. Sometimes they can overreact though so they must be kept in the loop and educated in what you want. With our ancestors it is more of a partnership than us dictating or ordering them.

The concept of your castle and realm is for illustration, you should now understand, because our ancestors show up in many different locations in our dreams. It is more accurate to say they visit our personal realms and they do not leave the spirit or dream world for our conscious world. Most cultures believe strongly in ancestor veneration; many of these cultures also try to connect with these, our strongest allies. Particularly this is true of the ori (soul) ancestors from earlier lives. I actually identified my principal and two guides before I started venerating my ancestors and that worked for me. I think most start with their blood ancestors and maybe that inhibits growth without the missing link of the ori ancestors...I am just speculating out loud with you.

8.7 The Dead

One of the toughest adjustments I had to make was not being scared of The Dead and that too is a process. In my case, I immediately saw the importance of the 24/7 principal guide we all have and the helping two to seven guides (who we now call ori ancestors). This made it easy for me to realize the importance of having advocates within The Dead and their substantial importance to my growth or education. Now that I am convinced these are ori ancestors, it might have been tougher for me to grow in my understanding of The Dead. However, if we agree that at the end of the day all our ancestors of every type are part of The Dead; it should not cause you too much apprehension. There is always going to be positives and negatives (balance) within The Dead. If you can somehow get over your fear, growth will come easy and quick.

The mistake (as I see it) most make is

shying away from The Dead rather than meeting them full on. Almost all of advanced study and growth involves The Dead. The Native Americans (and I include ALL of the Americas; not just North America) peoples recognize the importance of dreams and dream experts. I live in the same area as the famous author Carlos Castaneda's hero, Don Juan Matus lived. The Yaqui people's shamans are very astute on dreams. I began spending time with them about ten years ago. When I became a Lucumi Babalawo, I rekindled those relationships and shared with the Yaquis what I was learning. They had foreseen this and in fact my odu combination targeting primary education and this book! I recommend Mr. Castaneda's books, I have not read them all and I read them in my teens, but they do have value. Hopefully you are learning that my education and influences are primarily Lucumi, but with a healthy dose of Native American and India-Nepal- Tibet influences. You see my opinion is the mosaic is like a jigsaw puzzle, different cultures have different strengths and weaknesses. I try to connect the dots, build my picture or mosaic with pieces from several cultures; the pieces do not always fit, but I have been lucky and want you to benefit from me being just a bit further up the road from you.

We could delve deep into the mysticism of dreams, The Dead, moths, dragonflies, birds, fish, trees and ashe, but this book is a primer, an introduction to get you started. However, we will touch more on this in the next chapter along with Nature and ashe. My goal though is to build your foundation with less complex subjects than traveling within your dreams, to others dreams, finding your dream power animal etc. The Dead are complex and you must crawl before you can fly. It is a process; not a snap of the fingers. The Yaqui for example teach to find and focus on our hands, our feet, of a specific appendage in our dreams as a first step in advanced studies. The concept is to control the focus or focal point and grow. If you get to that point unaided, you have a gift for dream manipulations or what some call lucid dreaming. Perhaps one day I'll write a companion book for this primer on advanced studies; but I like teaching the basics as opposed to arguing with the "experts". Still I am proud of this book, and it should help you make at least a connection with your ancestors and allow you to enjoy the fruits of your labor, persistence and patience.

8.9 Communication

To close this chapter I want to share another example that might help you understand the process a little better. There are many types of communication and different forms all have strengths and weaknesses. Suppose you are speaking face to face; it is the best for understanding and one of the worst for both people remembering the same thing. The telephone is another strong mode where we can hear inflections; but for memory agreement by the two parties and long term remembering it is poor. Chat is very difficult and many misunderstandings arise. This can happen too in a written letter. What we are sharing here is a verbal or written message by you to an ancestor or member of The Dead. On the receiving side it is a message in a subconscious dream….not too easy to say the least. Be cognizant of this fact.

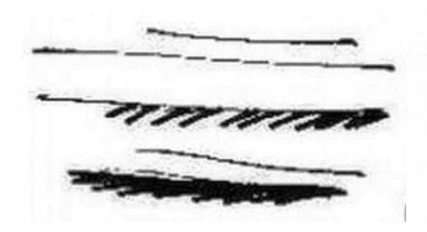

CHAPTER NINE

Core Concepts

9.0 Prelude: The Eagles Eye (Barbara Cromartie)

Before we dive into the core concepts I want to share an experience. Perhaps it is off topic or we can use it as a break. The reason I am sharing it is to reinforce the fact that there are other proven methods to see or commune with spirits other than the one I am teaching you. Dateline: 1987 (Six years before my first visit to Cuba). I was having a significant relationship with one of my great loves of this life. She with the big brain and great legs, my Chicago treasure continues to be a celebrity of note. She had the diversity to verbally joust with Mortimer Adler or advocate equality speaking in front of thousands. She I suppose still is a champion of the little guy and she was quite interested in various spiritualties. For five magical years I scratched my head wondering why she was wasting her time with me. Famous astrologers, occultists, spiritualists and religious leaders drew her attentions while I plodded on with what I thought were the real things that mattered in the conscious world. One winter's day I picked her up from an appointment at a small office on Michigan Avenue. She glided in to the waiting room after the assistant announced I was waiting. With her a beautiful lady who had a smile that lit up the room. I was introduced to Barbara Cromartie.

I was invited for a cup of coffee and we sat down. Barbara immediately said to me "You are the oldest of three children and a very old soul". "Huh?" I looked at my gal, raised an eyebrow and said to Barbara "So she has been sharing my secrets, has she!" My gal looked me in the eye and said "nope". My gal did not tell lies or fibs, so I was puzzled and then it dawned on me that this woman was a spiritualist. On the way home she insisted that she has not told Barbara about my family and she told me a bit about Barbara. My gal had been introduced to Barbara through Oprah who a few months before had grown to be nationally syndicated. Long before Chicago was even on the radar for Oprah (years before) Barbara predicted on air Oprah would relocate to Chicago and become the biggest star in television.

Despite my reservations, I had a dream that encouraged me to go visit Barbara and of course my gal was encouraging me too. I caved in and went for a session. The first time was jointly with my gal, and I seem to remember that Barbara grabbed both of my hands, closed her eyes for a few seconds, released my hands and started speaking normally to me. I continued to be quite skeptical and wary, but in retrospect all she said came true. She was not an oracle for all questions; most, but not all. Barbara would connect with someone or something to get the answers I assumed, but I never asked. Now, I am shocked I did not. Barbara traveled all over and only spent about a week every three months in Chicago. I assumed Oprah (who was now the huge success she had prophesized) and her growing inner circle took most of Barbara's time. My gal also became a regular, I was not a regular, nor was I invited to become a regular. Therefore, I did not see Barbara again until almost a year later.

On this occasion I went alone and again she was spot on accurate. In fact, she forecast my brother's death in a burning building a tragedy she said would change the world. This was in 1988 and my brother was murdered in the World Trade Center on September 11th 2001. Of course I warned my brother way back then, and it concerned him. It concerned him more after the World Trade Center bombing in 1993. By 1998 we started talking about a new career for him, me and two of our closest friends. It was a frequent topic of conversation amongst the four of us and we planned to act on it in 2002 or 2003. I went back to see Barbara a final time in 1989 or 1990 and her accuracy remained. I stopped seeing her because I was distressed and scared by my brother's prophesy and my relationship with my gal was ending.

The reason for the story is to make a few

points. The first is that I am not an oracle, seer, empathic, psychic or even the top priest of Orun in Lucumi. The second is that there are many methods to connect with the spirits and I do not know much about any. In fact I view my method I am sharing as something that I purposely stumbled across. Thirdly, my opinion is that you might need to make adjustments by trial and error with a healthy dose of patience. My hope is that the methods to connect and remember are helpful to everyone; I believe they will be if you are dedicated, patient and have an inquisitive mind.

9.1 Introduction

Perhaps I should have started with this chapter, but instead we will use the next two chapters to corral and hopefully simplify the many concepts we have discussed. These chapters are more for everyone regardless of your culture, spirituality or religion than my Lucumi brethren. Those who are Lucumi should already be running toward the finish line.

Latinos Native Americans, Indigenous Peoples, Indians, Chinese and other Eastern philosophy students should be approaching the finish line too. My non-Latino Christians, Muslims, Jews and European friends might need a bit more mortar with their foundation blocks before I can send them flying to the finish line. Like we discussed earlier if you happen to be a Buddhist, Pagan, drummer, dancer, naturalist, spiritualist, yoga or meditation student or a plethora of other avocations you might already be well on your way. Still, I think this wrapping of the package and adding the pretty bow in the next chapter might help you on your way.

While our focus is Ancestor Networking and connecting with The Dead, I think it is prudent to take a step back and discuss the importance of three core concepts we Lucumi embrace and how these are essential to our understanding. Yes, these are core building blocks or keys that are important to Ancestor Networking. The names of ashe and ori are really not important, other cultures call them other names. Other cultures may be slightly different, but most other cultures introduce these two important concepts and refer to them and their significance frequently. You might need to adjust them slightly to fit your culture, but you should at the very least recognize them and their importance as a foundation. The third core concepts are Nature and balance.

9.2 Ashe

Ashe (ase, ache axe) I think you understand (because we have used this concept throughout the book). Let's add some visuals for you to consider, James Cameron's epic film Avatar had its Tree of Souls. The Tree Of Souls is a concept that is found throughout Africa, India, Asia, America all over with indigenous cultures. Mr. Cameron did not make this up, nor did his cowriters; he embellished and borrowed the concept that we are connected with our ancestors, The Dead and Nature. The Yoruba call this connecting energy ashe, but maybe you missed the film, so let me share another. For Christians it would be the characters in the Arthurian legends like the Lady of the Lake, the elves Merlin lived with in his depression and there are many other examples in many cultures. One of the challenges is identifying all the schools of thought, hypothecs, philosophies, or even just identifying the many names connecting the soul, the body, and the spirits with Nature. Science continually alludes to this connection, but the connection details seem to elude scientists, the same is true of anthropologists. Metaphysical, hidden fibers, both shields and networks, charged platforms of energy; seriously the list is almost endless even for scholars. There are so many theories it is impossible to investigate them all. Therefore, I am not going to make all of these connections, you must or at least investigate the ones who appeal or you deem to have merit.

I chose ashe because not only is it ancient, it is one of the easier systems to explain in a couple of paragraphs. However understand that despite this simplicity it is as expansive and multilayered subject that is fathomless; no human will ever learn all there is to learn about it or our other core concepts. We can start anywhere, skip around and we will grow from it. Our narrowing of the concept of ashe was necessary or we would fall into that fathomless pit of knowledge. For us, discussing the basics of ashe and applying some of these basics to our ancestors and The Dead are useful. Therefore, even if your culture calls ashe something different, it should be included in your foundation and throughout your development. The same is true of the concept of ori (loosely defined as soul, that which "goes on"). The third major concept is Nature (both seen and unseen). How these three concepts interact between themselves is important. Once we have a basic understanding of the three concepts and how they interact then we can apply these relationships to our ancestors and The Dead, both consciously when we are awake, but also in the subconscious when we are dreaming.

9.4 Ori

Ori we have discussed and compared to the soul or atman. It is what "goes on" after death claims our body. In the Lucumi system it is more than just the soul or atman; we call it the divine spirit. One reason we call it this is almost 100% of humans do not communicate with Olodumare, Olorun or Olofin until their host body dies and ori is judged by Olorun. Therefore if you are alive and reading this know you do have a chance to communicate with Olofin, but only 1 in 256 humans have this chance. The one is if your ruling odu is otura sa that is one of the 256 odu that answer questions like this or destiny. If you happen to be an awo (priest of Orunmila) you would immediately have a 3 in 256 chance and if you completed your training after five years of service you might receive the ceremonial knife and then you would gain a fourth odu and have a 4 in 256 chance. If you happened to receive Olofin (our top rank in Lucumi) you would automatically have this possibility. But (and it is a big but) all this means is you gain the possibility to communicate with Olofin and no certainty, no guarantee, just the possibility. I have otura sa in my odu scheme, I earned it with my knife, but Olofin has never reached out to me... and I would be surprised if he did.

For those of you outside of any branch of West African system you would still have a 1 on 256 chance of communicating with God (whatever your God(s) is. God may hear or receive your messages and pleas; but there is no guarantee God will answer you or engage in a conversation with you. In the unlikely event God does wish to engage you in conversation, God obviously can do this in a dream or while you are wide awake in an unaltered state. Now at least you understand why we call ori our divine spirit.

Ori has a relationship with not only God(s), but Orishas or immortals of whatever spirituality you have. I personally have never seen or heard of an Orisha (or any immortal) appearing in the conscious world in their full glory. I have seen many times them mount or inhabit a human and speak and act through the human. Lucumi tambores are where this usually takes place, but I have personally seen it elsewhere too. More commonly I have seen and had in - depth conversations (as I shared in an earlier chapter) in the dream world or on the astral planes with a few

Orishas. To be honest I do not know if Orishas have the capability to communicate with us outside of the examples I cited. I do think it is possible, but never witnessing it or hearing of it from a reliable source makes me unsure.

Ori is another of the main concepts that is simple to understand generally, but extremely deep to master. I do not know or believe any human masters the intricacies of ori (or the soul, atman etc.) My belief is that ori does connect with we humans but it seems (at least to me) that ori is not something we can tap or use like an oracle more like A) Ori knows, sees and records every aspect of our being while it inhabits us. B) Ori does occasionally share glimpses of other bodies it inhabited. Most notably of these are our ori ancestors (what I used to believe were simply our 2 -7 spiritual guides and our 24/7 principle guide. Channeling through these we can access other Dead spirits in the subconscious dream world or in an altered state of consciousness. Regarding other ancestors (blood, DNA, or lineage) I do not currently think ori is as active in providing a connection; yet I am certain ori records all it sees, hears and contacts.

Connecting with ori is not really the subject of this book, but it is a connection and a concept that we should not undervalue or ignore. Many agree that in the big picture our ori is much more important than the body we are living in. The Lucumi believe strongly that anyone can access ori and it does not require a ceremony to do so. The Nigerian Yoruba access ori through ceremony thus is costs, much like their egbe ceremony to access egbe. In Lucumi as we have discussed accessing our spiritual guides for both The Dead and our blood ancestors is free. Does the ori or egbe ceremony have any benefits other than the Lucumi free access? There are none that I have seen, nor any that I have recognized despite many discussions with priests and luminaries in the Nigerian IFA community.

9.5 For my Lucumi Friends

You've read almost the whole book now and not a word has been said of the elephant in the room, blood sacrifice. The reason I have not included it to this point if for other cultures it is controversial (to say the least). Olodumare, Olorun and Olofin though protect all cultures, not just our own. Other cultures do not see that we eat what we kill 98% of the time, or that priests are supposed to be trained in compassion in how to kill without pain and animal husbandry to honor what we kill. Cultures like Christianity, Islam and Hinduism all used and approved of blood sacrifice until the last hundred years. None of this will matter to a PETA member or a Buddhist or Jain, they will turn away and castigate Lucumi and Yoruba for our practice of blood sacrifice.

Part of this disapproval is of our own making. We allowed and some ile and houses still allow under - educated and untrained priests and lesser members. Some of these become independents with no ile or house and have no or little education and training, they fester like a cancer. Many of these continue to develop warped ideas and promote blood sacrifice without really understanding it. Some even crown or make other priests without ever earning ashe through ceremony. Part of this problem comes from malicious fraud and other from people receiving fake ashe through pseudo priests. The fact of the matter is in our many traditions we bestow ashe through ceremony and give rank before it is earned. This worked fine in the villages of West Africa hundreds of years ago, but it does not work well in today's world that includes The Diaspora. Tourist priests may be given real ashe from a venerable lineage, but when they are not trained or educated for years (six days a week) they should not be allowed to have clients. When they have clients it reflects poorly on the ile or house. Thus we have the first major problem.

The second major problem is that under trained and under educated priests and followers do not understand sacrifice, they overuse blood sacrifice for ebbo and all kinds of things. There are many types of sacrifice that are not blood. To solve minor problems, desires or offerings with blood is like killing an ant with a bazooka. In fact it is disrespectful. The wise, well-educated and trained know this and practice it. They are creative in their sacrifice and this often means saving a blood sacrifice for when it is appropriate, not for every solution. Of course as a Baba Awo I use blood sacrifice; but I do not overuse it like many do. It is a bit like taking an antibiotic such as ampicillin, if we use it every time we have a cold, fever or belly ache it becomes less effective. The same is true with divination by the under trained, they use it all the time. They over use it because they are undertrained and have nowhere else to turn and then get something out of a "How To" book that maybe does not even explain the difference of an odu in ire or osogbo! It is incredible to me how the undertrained fail to realize they are not experts in all things whatever their rank or tenure is. This is the second problem of our own making.

The third problem is Nature and its importance in our culture, this cannot be minimized, circumvented or ignored. Show me a Lucumi priest who ignores this cornerstone of our culture and I will show you a priest who was not trained properly. Look at it this way if you throw your ebbo to the sea in a plastic bag is Yemaya or Olokun going to reward you for the pollution of the bag? Will Oshun listen as you pollute her rivers? Osian be cooperative when you litter plastic on a tree or near the roots of one of his trees? Part of being a wise priest is using your own head to find solutions. If you run into a vexing problem then you can and should be asking for help from The Dead, your ancestors, orishas or Orunmila. Those who are well educated and trained see this; those who are not are blind. The main thought here is: Do not kill a flea on your arm with a bazooka or you will lose your arm in the process. Don't claim to be an expert when you are not if you love our culture, because when you do, it hurts our culture. When Esu and Iku take our ori to Olorun to be judged we cannot fool them or trick them into ignoring our indiscretions and crimes, they see all; so do not jeopardize ori if you are wise.

9.8 Nature

There is an old expression: "Never underestimate the power of Nature". You do not need to be a tree hugger to agree that humans are made from Nature, a part of Nature and need Nature to exist. Many cultures including Orishas are deeply rooted in Nature; the concept of ashe is interwoven in Nature. Nature is also an avenue to our ancestors and The Dead because the spirits came from Nature as humans and continue to be connected to Nature as spirits. The Lucumi and Yoruba as well as almost every culture use Nature as a cure (ebbo); in fact there are no cures or ebbo I can think of that do not include Nature.

Similar to how we acquire ashe often through Nature and natural things we can use Nature to enhance or improve our connection with ancestors and The Dead. I touched upon having Nature as a part of your shrine and this is important. The better our connection to Nature the easier and stronger are our connections with ancestors and The Dead, it is that simple. The mechanics of this are also fairly simple build your connection with Nature and you will reap the rewards. The fastest and easiest way to acquire ashe is to make a gift to Nature, such as planting a tree, cleaning a section of a river, the beach or a forest. Do this as often as you like it will always reward you with ashe and the more ashe we have the easier it is to connect with our ancestors and The Dead, simple!

I should also point out that when you litter, pollute or abuse Nature you pay a penalty, your ashe is reduced depending on the severity of your crime. We continue to talk about balance and this is another important example. The bottom line is unless you are contributing to Nature you can almost forget about making a connection with your ancestors or The Dead.

We also spoke earlier about altered states of consciousness and I'd like to finish this chapter with this. Clearly doing meditation or yoga in Nature (or even better in a place of natural power) will help you make a connection or advances in your study. The same is true of other altered states.

9.9 Altered States of Consciousness

Like I shared earlier this is a more complex and diverse area of advanced studies. I also reiterated that I am certainly not an expert in any of these. I suggested if you are a student of these to have a discussion or give this book to your guru or teacher and they probably have major contributions to your growth and making or strengthening a connection. However this book is about dreaming with or networking with our ancestors and The Dead in or through our dreams.

The point I want to make in this chapter is it is possible to use any altered state as a vehicle or substitution for the astral planes or dream world. Yet any of these altered states can also work in concert with our dreams as well. The fact is that these disciplines of altered states can all be useful in building or improving your connections. It is similar to when we speak more than one language fluidly it is much easier and quicker to speak a third language well. The individual that speaks but one language almost always has a difficult and long road speaking, reading and writing a second language.

Please allow me to make an off topic comment. Why, because it is something that I am often embarrassed by. The sad fact is most people who know only one language are the harsh critics of an accent or an error by the nonnative. Natives who speak more than their own native tongue tend to be compassionate and encouraging.

EPILOUGE :

Like I said throughout the book thbook. is is a primer, not a complete works, it is a process for you and for me. Some might feel I am not sharing enough and I understand that criticism. I wish I had all the answers, but hopefully you are further along and have a better understanding of where and how to get where you are going after reading my book. If you require more, I am always happy to interact with my readers and I share how in the subsequent pages.

I can tell you that listening to my ancestors in my dreams has changed my life and to be frank made me much less concerned about when I "go on". I no longer worry about death because I am not afraid of it, for me it is another adventure.

Very Special Thanks

Cover Photos: Pete McBride Photography, first published in *National Geographic*

Interior Illustrations: Sr. Victario Evelio Cue Villate

ANCESTOR NETWORKING

Works by Charles Spencer King

Nature's Ancient Religion: Orisha worship & IFA.

Ifa y los Orishas: La Religion Antigua de la Naturaleza

Havana My Kind of Town

Ancestor Networking (espanol version viene)

The Adventures of Asabi & Ropo: The Native Americans

Traveling Lite

The Bronze Plaques of Geneva

Fidel is Coming Y Fidel Viene: a screenplay

Ifa and Orisha Reverence: Avoiding Fraud, Charlatans and Scams en route to Truth , Power & Wisdom (espanol version abril 2016)

ANCESTOR NETWORKING

Find me on Facebook and these groups and pages:

Divine Intervention
Info Lucumi
IFA and Orisha Poetry~ poesía de la IFA y Orisha devoción

Free articles at
Academia.com
Charles Spencer King

My Services

Nogales Consultation: 90 min. Individual Session over a meal 500; Group 300 per person

Nogales Weekend: Individual Session Sat 6 hours, Sun 6 hours 2500; Group 1500 per person

Your Location Consultation 90 min. Individual Session over a meal 1500; Group 800 per person

Your Location Weekend: Individual Session, Sat 6 hours, Sun 6 hours 3500; Group 2000 per person

Havana: Four six hour days 3500; Group 2000 per person (limit 5)

Havana: Seven six hour days 5000; Group 2500 per person (limit 5)

My Terms

Nogales sessions are either in Nogales Az, Mexico. Tubac Golf Resort & Spa + 200 + Sedan and driver RT

Nogales, AZ Airport: Runway 7199 x 100ft (asphalt); Commercial, Tucson
Links: http://www.tubacgolfresort.com/
Mex: http://www.hotelfraymarcos.com/

Your Location: I am FOB Nogales, Mex; Sedan and Driver to and from Tucson; Business Class Air; Hotel and Food First Class/ Superior, Deluxe/ Luxury or Resort*; for Mexico, US, Canada and Caribbean; Surcharge for other locations.

Havana: FOB Nogales, Mex; Business Class Air; 250 CUC per diem (including travel days). Havana is a deal because I love it and I have my own place and transportation there.

* Unless you are in an exotic location, I prefer a hotel to staying with you. In Havana, I may invite you over; but not for the night.

ANCESTOR NETWORKING

Made in the USA
Middletown, DE
08 September 2016